Praise for

THE INNOVATOR'S SPIRIT

"In *The Innovator's Spirit*, readers will learn that now more than ever before, encouraging innovation and recognizing disruptive threats are paramount to long-term success. Chuck provides valuable insights about how to understand what is necessary for capturing and maintaining your Innovator's Spirit. This is a must-read for any business leader."

—ROBERT INGRAM, retired Chairman and CEO of
Glaxo Wellcome

"*The Innovator's Spirit* gives us the gift of the evolution of a true innovator's mind and his accumulated wisdom and experience from leading, as CEO, an innovative company. Chuck tackles the extraordinary challenge of how you scale innovation by multiplying innovators who have the talents and beliefs to overcome the natural obstacles that tend to favor stability over turbulence."

—GERALD D. BELL, PhD, Founder and CEO of Bell Leadership
Institute and *New York Times* best-selling author

"Everyone *doesn't* get a trophy. In *The Innovator's Spirit*, Swoboda delivers the key traits common among innovators and innovative organizations. He captivates readers by weaving his own experiences in leading a high-growth tech company with stories of iconic innovators and their innovations. This is an inspiring guide for anyone, from those with the courage and ideas to change the world to the ones who already have."

—**NEAL HUNTER,** Serial Entrepreneur and co-Founder, former Chairman, and CEO of Cree, Inc.

"Rules and process kill innovation. However, conventional management teaches us that rules and process are needed to grow and scale a business. In *The Innovator's Spirit*, Chuck Swoboda lays out with candor and clarity how you don't have to sacrifice one for the other and that it's in the best interest of organizations to cultivate and protect the leadership mindset and spirit needed to solve complex problems. This is a must-read for anyone looking to solve an impossible problem and provides real world-changing value."

—**JIM WHITEHURST,** President and CEO of Red Hat

"*The Innovator's Spirit* provides a tangible portfolio of personal leadership practices and assets, including the power of purposeful imagination, relentless conviction, and relationship synergy, that embody the Spirit that is the unapologetic pursuit of a better way."

—**DARREN JACKSON,** former CEO of Advance Auto Parts and CFO of Best Buy

"*The Innovator's Spirit* is a must-read for anyone trying to transform an organization. It outlines how a leader can foster a culture of risk-taking while allowing the organization to learn from its failures. Chuck Swoboda's insights and experiences driving an innovative mindset are truly inspirational."

—**MICHAEL LOVELL,** PhD, President of Marquette University

"In *The Innovator's Spirit*, Chuck Swoboda reminds us that real innovation is about being a pragmatic idealist—to have the focus and the will to pursue what seems implausible while constantly understanding that nothing matters without commercial success and a broader purpose that can move the world forward."

—**ANTHONY TJAN**, *New York Times* best-selling author, entrepreneur, and venture capitalist

"A frontline view of how organizations innovate to win, Chuck Swoboda tests your core beliefs and reframes them in ways that unleash your Innovator's Spirit. I witnessed these ideas in practice with incredible outcomes that changed the LED industry."

—**TOM WERNER**, Chairman and CEO at SunPower Inc.

"Rapid change and disruption are necessary for success in most industries today. *The Innovator's Spirit* offers an insightful, compelling, and candid platform for today's leaders to reflect on and fuel their own innovative spirit. Telling the story of one of the most innovative companies in America, Swoboda beautifully and simply challenges us to think and act differently as we strive to create value in an increasingly complex world. Swoboda's story makes risk and failure incredibly attractive norms for anyone wanting to bring meaning and life to their work. *The Innovator's Spirit* is a joy to read; one can't help but want to drive change after perusing the first few chapters!"

—**KRISTINA M. ROPELLA**, PhD, Opus Dean of Engineering at Marquette University

"Engaging . . . raw and real . . . practical and inspiring—this book on innovation is a standout. Chuck Swoboda has written a great how-to book, portraying the best innovators as misfits, underdogs, and even pirates. He shows us how to leverage dissatisfaction into innovation. Enjoy!"

—**BETTY NOONAN**, Executive Vice President and Chief Growth Officer at nVent Inc.

"Innovation is *the* key part of any successful business. My father started Trek in a small barn with three employees. Today, one of the ways we evaluate leaders at Trek is their ability to see something bigger than the barn. My father had that ability, and we want every leader at Trek to have it too. *The Innovator's Spirit* can help you see something bigger whether you are a product manager, an engineer, or work in the finance department."

—**JOHN BURKE,** President, Trek Bicycle Corporation

DISCOVER THE MINDSET TO PURSUE THE IMPOSSIBLE

THE
INNOVATOR'S
SPIRIT

CHUCK SWOBODA

FAST
COMPANY
Press

Fast Company Press
New York, New York
www.fastcompanypress.com

This work is being published under the Fast Company Press imprint by an exclusive arrangement with Fast Company. Fast Company and the Fast Company logo are registered trademarks of Mansueto Ventures, LLC. The Fast Company
Press logo is a wholly owned trademark of Mansueto Ventures, LLC.

Distributed by Greenleaf Book Group

For ordering information or special discounts for bulk purchases, please contact Greenleaf Book Group at PO Box 91869, Austin, TX 78709, 512.891.6100.

Design and composition by Greenleaf Book Group
Cover design by Greenleaf Book Group

Publisher's Cataloging-in-Publication data is available.

Print ISBN: 978-1-7324391-6-0

eBook ISBN: 978-1-7324391-7-7

Part of the Tree Neutral® program, which offsets the number of trees consumed in the production and printing of this book by taking proactive steps, such as planting trees in direct proportion to the number of trees used: www.treeneutral.com

Printed in the United States of America on acid-free paper

20 21 22 23 24 25 26   10 9 8 7 6 5 4 3 2 1

First Edition

For my parents, who instilled the belief that you can accomplish anything you set your mind to.

For my wife, who has been my best friend and partner every day on this incredible journey called life.

CONTENTS

A Test of Spirit

AS I STOOD IN FRONT of several hundred employees in the company gym on my last day as CEO, a role I had held for the past sixteen years, I was filled with a range of emotions. These were my friends, colleagues, coworkers, and teammates. They were my second family. I was proud of what we had accomplished and sad that I wouldn't be leading the team anymore. I also felt a sense of relief, knowing that I was going to get a break from the pressure of running a public company. Hovering above these emotions was a feeling of regret—regret that the company we had built was changing. The "magic" that had made our company special, that enabled our growth from a start-up to a global technology company, had slipped away. And I had let it slip away. I had lost my innovator's spirit.

My journey of learning what innovation is and what drives it began in 1993 when I joined Cree, a small LED (light-emitting diode) company in North Carolina that revolutionized the way people think about light. At first, I served on the frontlines. I worked in roles ranging from marketing, sales, and customer service to quality, manufacturing, and human resources. Eventually, I was promoted to president, chief operating officer, and ultimately to CEO. Our team commercialized the blue LED, created the first lighting-class LEDs, developed new classes of semiconductor devices that enable electric vehicles and 5G wireless networks, and brought LED light bulbs into the mainstream. We were awarded more than five thousand patents covering a range of inventions and many innovations. I was proud to be part of that incredible innovation engine. Over the course of my twenty-five-year career at Cree, I worked closely with our development teams, where I became the co-inventor on twenty-five patents. It was a blast.

But in my last few years at Cree, something felt different. I had begun to shift the beliefs and behaviors that I had embraced when I first started there. As the company became bigger and more successful, the stakes seemed to grow larger. And so did the weight on my shoulders. It became much more important to avoid making mistakes so we could hit our financial targets—especially since we were a publicly traded company. While we were willing to break the rules early on in our single-minded pursuit of innovation, after more than a decade as CEO, I felt pressured to dial it back and deliver more predictable results. That's what the shareholders were demanding.

In our pursuit of something better, we took risks and experienced failures along the way to go with great successes. When things went right, it was expected. But when things went wrong, it was my fault—and the cumulative memory of failure built over time. There's an analogy in golf that as you get older, your putting ability gets worse. Some people say you lose your nerve, because you remember all of the putts you've missed. Over time, it seemed like I started to lose my nerve and become afraid of failure. I spent more and more of my time sitting in meetings trying to optimize best practices rather than think beyond them. That mindset changed the kind of people I hired. Rather than hunt for innovators, I brought on people to help us manage our risk. I was playing not to lose—while doing my best to ensure that we delivered our quarterly results. My priority was to our shareholders, not driving innovation. I had forgotten that innovation is what had created value for the shareholders in the first place.

The company was doing fine, but we had lost the magic, and I was miserable. At some point the stress got to me, and my health suffered. Quite literally, I needed a break, so I resigned. It was time for a new leader to guide the company on the next phase of its journey. While I didn't completely realize it at the time, stepping away from Cree helped me gain the perspective I needed to write this book. My behaviors and beliefs had become clouded by everything I had once tried to avoid. I had been trying to manage innovation instead of leading it. Leaving the company allowed me to look back and explore why we had been so successful at what we did. I also realized that I would not have been considered an innovator when I first joined the company. I had no idea what that really meant at the time.

THE BENEFITS OF HINDSIGHT

Rewinding a bit, I began my career as an engineer at Hewlett-Packard (HP), a company that was started in a garage in Palo Alto, California—when Silicon Valley was still mostly fruit orchards. At the time, HP was considered one of the most innovative companies in the world. I had an indomitable belief that there was always a right or correct answer and a drive to find it. I had always been curious and liked solving problems. I could accept risk—what was the big deal?

Then Cree came calling. The company had just invented the world's first blue LED—then considered the holy grail of lighting. While it was far from market-ready, it held the promise of enabling LED applications that might just make the ubiquitous incandescent bulb obsolete. That was exciting stuff for a young engineer like me to think about.

The company flew me out to North Carolina to spend a day with the founders, where I got to hear about the incredibly innovative things they were doing. Although they were very secretive— they wouldn't even let me in the building—it was still intoxicating being around people who were working on things that many people thought were just theories or simply not possible. In fact, at that time, one of the executives at HP, a famous LED inventor, publicly stated that what Cree was trying to do simply couldn't be done. That was part of the excitement—taking on the challenge to prove others wrong. Now, with the help of hindsight, I can see that what Cree was doing was truly innovation in action.

But when Cree first offered me a job, I said no. Given that I had a solid job, a new house, and a young family to support, it seemed too risky. There were too many unknowns. I was being asked to give up what I had, what was real, for something that might be better—but that also could be nothing. What I didn't realize at the time was that in school and on the job, I had been trained to control and eliminate risk—and Cree was too big of a leap for me to take at the time.

I continued to pursue my career at HP and watch Cree from afar, as they went public and gained a reputation as a company on the cutting edge of innovation. I started doubting my earlier decision. Cree seemed like a place I wanted to be part of—an entrepreneurial culture that was the polar opposite of the highly managed environment I commuted to every day at HP. I began to see my career at HP approaching a crossroads. I was frustrated with the system and the management processes of a large company. I didn't like being told to follow the rules and be patient. I was jaded by the fact that the values that had made the company great—what the founders called the "HP Way"—no longer really applied. I thought about going back to school, either to get my MBA or to become a patent attorney.

Then, I received a call from one of the Cree founders. He asked me for my address because he had something he wanted to send me. He told me to "just read it" and let him know what I thought. The next day, I received an express package with a job offer inside. It didn't specify much more than what my salary would be and that I was mostly on my own for relocation expenses. Cree was calling again—they wanted me on their team. The catch was that they wanted an answer in two days.

I was excited—I wanted to say yes—but I hadn't completely shaken my earlier worries. I remember calling my dad and asking him for advice. He said: "Son, you work for one of the best companies in the world. It seems awfully risky. I'm not sure I would do it." Ugh. Sound advice, but not what I was hoping for.

I also discussed the opportunity with my wife, Karen, and she gave me some of the best advice of my life. She flipped the question around on me: "What happens if you don't do it? You'll spend the rest of your life wondering, 'What if?'"

She then asked me to consider the worst case. If things didn't work out at Cree, could I get another job? I knew I could. Would I learn some new skills by taking the job? "Without a doubt," I said.

She looked at me and said: "Then take the job. I don't want to live with someone who's going to spend the rest of their life questioning what might have been."

Those were powerful words. What I didn't realize at the time was that Karen was the true innovator in our family.

Two weeks later, I packed our car with some clothes and drove from Colorado to North Carolina to take a job I didn't know much about. Karen, who was pregnant at the time and caring for our four-year-old daughter, would have to wait to follow until we sold our house.

Taking the job at Cree helped me connect with the behaviors and beliefs that all innovators possess. As I worked hand-in-hand with our team of innovators, I evolved as a person—and as a leader. I learned to embrace those beliefs and behaviors that, in time, empowered me to attack the rules of the management world, to overcome my training and habits, and to do something truly new and innovative. I learned to go beyond just finding the correct answer to focusing on chasing bigger ideas and outcomes instead—to go beyond the boundaries that merely result in more of the same.

Cree was built on a strategy of innovation: to create new things that delivered value to our customers. But to execute that strategy, we needed to develop people who could lead innovation and scale with the company. That became our biggest challenge. Bright, talented people were getting stuck on a set of behaviors and habits that prevented them from moving ahead. I would sit down and have conversations with them about how they had to change their approach. They would nod their heads and agree to try, only to be back in my office a few weeks later struggling with the same problem. This was frustrating for all of us. When I asked them if they had tried the different behaviors that we had talked about, they would say, "Yes, well, kind of." As we continued to talk, it would always become clear that while they fully intended to change, they would eventually fall back on the same habits that were driven by their core beliefs. As soon as things got busy and the pressure got turned up, they would resort to a set of behaviors that were counter to innovation leadership.

A JOURNEY OF REDISCOVERY

My goal in writing this book is to help you uncover your own innovator's spirit—or to find it again if you've lost it—using my experience as your guide. My journey to recapture the spark that leads to disruptive innovation began a few years ago when I was invited to give a talk to a group of engineering students and faculty at Marquette University, my alma mater. A big theme of my speech was that innovation needed to be led—it couldn't be managed. After the speech, I was invited to lunch with a few of the administrators of the engineering program. They told me that they had started an innovation leadership program for the students, and they wondered if I would be willing to review the syllabus and materials for the course. I said yes.

I spent the next month reviewing the materials and making furious notations. Some of the material was spot-on. But more of it wasn't—much of the material smacked of academic theory written by a professor—not hard-earned lessons from the frontlines by someone who had seen innovation in action. They were arguing that innovation could be boiled down into a neat process—which ran counter to everything I had experienced in my career.

While they hadn't really asked for it, I ended up writing pages and pages of thoughts and reactions that I eventually handed over to the team at Marquette. I'm sure they hadn't expected much. But to their credit, they wanted more: more insights, more perspective, and especially, more stories. In fact, they told me that I should write a book. Now it was my turn to be blown away. Write a book? It had never occurred to me, but maybe they were on to something.

This book is the result of my commitment to rediscover my own innovator's spirit. By watching innovators in action in my own career, and by reading and researching the histories of many other disruptive innovators, I developed a series of connected behaviors and beliefs that all great innovators possess. But a word of caution: This isn't a how-to manual. Other books about innovation tend to focus on sharing what I think of as "recipes" for how to generate innovation inside organizations starved for that kind of thinking. Yet, by that very definition, you can't innovate if you're simply following the blueprint someone else has laid out. You'll just get the same result. That's why it's not the chef who follows the recipe that innovates—it's the one who combines ingredients in new and sometimes counterintuitive ways to get a mouth-watering dish that's never been made before.

It's why I generally don't read books on innovation. Because I believe they often lack the most important elements for innovation: your beliefs and mindset. This book is different. It is about going beyond the recipe to understand the ingredients and find your innovator's spirit. I hope you enjoy it.

It's Personal

*"We must accept finite disappointment,
but never lose infinite hope."*
—**Martin Luther King Jr.**

EVERYONE WANTS INNOVATIVE THINKING THESE days. To create new products and services. To find new customers and markets. To work smarter, not harder. To stay ahead of the competition. Innovation isn't optional; it's an imperative. If you don't innovate, you're dead in the water.

This book tackles an aspect about innovation that often gets overlooked: Innovation is personal. It's about people. It's not about a process or a system. It's a mindset, a belief that anything is possible—and you'll stop at nothing to make it happen. Innovation requires leadership and a burning desire to find a way to solve the problem or get to the goal, even if you seem to be the only one who recognizes it. You know there must be a better way and you're willing to do what it takes. It's about someone's emotions, character, and willingness to get their hands dirty—their spirit.

The innovator's spirit powers you to keep going, even when everyone else tells you to stop—to double down on your efforts because you can see something no one else can. If you don't keep pressing on, who else will make the impossible possible? That's what I consider innovation. That's what I consider fun.

Discovering your innovator's spirit is a journey. And it never ends. The innovator's spirit is built on a foundation of core beliefs that drive the behaviors of people like you and me to innovate by overcoming the obstacles that conventional thinking puts in our way. It's a passion rooted in wanting to do something that has never been done before, to solve problems that have never been solved, and to run through walls and leap over tall buildings to get there.

UNCOVERING YOUR INNOVATOR'S SPIRIT

I believe an innate innovator's spirit resides in all of us. It has been my experience, however, that not only can a person lose this spirit, but there are also those who can't tap into it. They either don't encounter a need for it, or they simply can't uncover it because it is buried under years of teaching and training that create beliefs and behaviors that don't lead to innovation. They've become conditioned to accept predictable results. Most people want order, they prefer the predictable and the routine, and there's absolutely nothing wrong with this. It should even be celebrated. It just won't result in innovation.

People who love to innovate, on the other hand, believe predictability is boring. True innovation is about leading—it's about embracing the beliefs and behaviors that inspire you and others to do something you didn't think was possible. What I have learned through the help of my executive coach, Dr. Gerald Bell, is that behaviors are tied to a set of core beliefs, and people fundamentally act based on those beliefs. What they really believe—not what they say they believe—is what drives their behavior, especially when under pressure or in a stressful situation. Sure, when someone is focused and thinking about a specific approach, you might be able to get some short-term behavior change. But when the pressure is on, people react, and their actions are driven by their beliefs. It's unconscious, like an autopilot. Until you change your beliefs, you can never adopt the behaviors that are core to the innovator's spirit. That's why innovation can't be a process. If you try to just copy the behaviors, you'll run into what a friend of mine calls "logical fallacies." Which is why just dressing and talking like Steve Jobs doesn't equate to leading innovation. You have to start with your beliefs.

Looking back, I recognize that discovering my own innovator's spirit began on a basketball court.

I was on a call discussing my upcoming visit to interview at Cree with Neal Hunter, one of the founders. Just as I was about to hang up the phone, he said, "Do me a favor and bring your basketball shoes. We play basketball at lunch." While I was a bit taken aback by the strange request, I said OK and told him I would bring my sneakers with me. I thought the request was unusual but also intriguing. What kind of company played basketball with their interview candidates?

Sure enough, after we spent the morning talking in the booth of a local restaurant, eight of us piled into cars and headed to a local gym. Once we got dressed and hit the court, we chose teams by shooting free throws. The first four people to make their shot would form the first team. It wasn't exactly pretty watching everyone shoot. We were a motley crew. Most of us were engineers—many had PhDs. No one was going to mistake us for elite athletes. None of us even played basketball in high school. Fortunately, I was young and tall. I figured I would do fine. It was just a pickup game, right? Wrong.

When the game started, I was blown away. Early on, as I dribbled the ball into the lane on my way to the hoop, I felt a jab in my side. Someone had just elbowed me! It was clear nothing was going to be easy. The play was intense. Players called their own fouls, but there was a sense of pride in calling only the most flagrant hacks. What these guys lacked in talent they were making up for in their will to win. I quickly found myself out of breath. But I wasn't going to let my teammates down, so I continued to hustle back on defense even as the sweat poured off my face and my lungs felt like they were going to burst.

What I realize now is that the team learned more about me on that basketball court than from any of the discussions we had earlier that day. My core beliefs and behaviors were on display. I wasn't thinking; I was just reacting. They could see whether I stood up for myself or backed down. Or whether I would dive for a loose ball even when I was out of gas. They also saw what kind of teammate I was. Was I someone who just shot the ball as soon as I touched it, or did I look to pass to the open man? Was I willing to set a pick and get slammed into to free up a teammate? What was I willing to do to help my team win?

At the same time, I could see how the other players behaved and what they believed in. You can learn so much about what someone believes based on how they act on a basketball court. What I didn't completely realize at the time was that many of those same behaviors are tied to the beliefs that drive innovation. It's not about the power of skills; it's about willpower.

I must have made a good impression that day because they offered me the job. After I joined the Cree team, we continued the tradition that if someone happened to be interviewing for a job when there was a game on, we'd ask them to play. While it wasn't an intentional strategy, it became a way for us to find people who were willing to compete, do what it takes, and adapt to changing situations—all of which the game of basketball provides. We weren't looking for how well someone dribbled or shot the ball. In some cases, we had players who had never been on a basketball court in their lives.

That didn't matter because we wanted to see how they adjusted to an unexpected situation. Were they willing to step outside of their comfort zone and try? Were they willing to put themselves at risk to see what happened? We also wanted to see their spirit, passion, enthusiasm, and desire as they played. Our goal was to find people who wanted to compete, no matter how well they played. We wanted people who cared about winning as a team—and were willing to do whatever they could to help the team. We wanted people who made the team better. Those are the signs of someone with the potential to uncover their innovator's spirit—signs we might not be able to identify any other way, especially not from a resume.

We had a few occasions where someone declined to play with us. Or, if they did play, they exhibited the kinds of selfish behaviors that were immediate red flags. I remember one guy who stayed close to the hoop rather than running back on defense. He scored a lot of points that day, but it was about him scoring and not helping his team win. He was "me first" instead of "team first." If you don't want someone to be your teammate on the basketball court, why would you want to hire them to be part of your innovation team?

A PATTERN OF BELIEFS AND BEHAVIORS

Obviously, I won't get the chance to face off with many of you on the basketball court. But that's not the only way to help assess where someone is on their journey to uncover their innovator's spirit. My intention is to ask you some tough questions in the following pages that, based on how you react, will tell you a lot about what you believe when it comes to innovation.

What I've learned in rediscovering my own innovator's spirit is that there are a set of connected beliefs and behaviors that great innovators possess—or are at least open-minded enough to embrace. These were the very things I had begun to ignore or overlook as I lost my innovator's spirit.

I remember when, as CEO of Cree, I was invited to speak at a young professionals event over breakfast. The room was filled with a few hundred eager and bright minds hungry for advice and wisdom. Many of them might have also hoped to land a job at Cree. It was a great opportunity to run an experiment.

As a way to wake everyone up before my speech, I asked them to partake in a ten-minute exercise. I told them to work with the other people at their table to solve the problem I was going to give them. I also asked them not to pull out their phones to google the answer. Once I had their attention, I posed the challenge I wanted them to solve: "How many barbers are there in New York City?"

There might have been some audible gasps from the audience. I saw more than a few faces that were staring back at me as if to say, "Did I hear you right? What kind of question is that?" I had clearly thrown them a curveball. After I confirmed that I did indeed want them to tell me the number of barbers in New York City, I looked at the clock and said, "You have ten minutes. Get started!"

I wandered around the room, listening to the conversations at the different tables. Once the ten minutes were up, I went back to the front of the room and asked to see a show of hands. "How many of you thought the question was so silly, you ignored it to talk among yourselves?" About one-third of the hands went up. "OK," I said. "How many of you started to work on the question but gave up when you determined that you didn't have enough information to work with?" This time, about half the hands in the room went up. "Finally," I said, "how many of you actually came up with an answer?" The remaining twenty percent of hands went up. "Before I give you the right answer," I told the audience, "I'd like to tell you that this is an actual interview question we ask at Cree. And for those of you who ignored it or who gave up, I'm not sure you'd like to work with us. But for those of you who fought through and came up with an answer, let me know if you ever want a new challenge. We'd love to talk with you about joining our team."

The point of asking the question was never to get a precise answer—it was a test of their innovator's spirit. To see if they had the will and the curiosity to try and fight through an unexpected situation. It's known as a "Fermi question," named for the famed physicist Enrico Fermi, who helped develop the atomic bomb. At Cree, we developed a reputation for asking hard questions like these of everyone we interviewed—something that rubbed some people the wrong way. I even had one of our human resources managers complain to me that we weren't hiring enough people because the questions were too hard. She was frustrated that in some departments we typically hired only one of every one hundred candidates the human resources team brought in for interviews. She was missing the point. Our goal wasn't to hire just anyone. It was to hire people who had the innovator's spirit—regardless of their role in the company. Whether someone worked in finance or human resources, sales or operations, we wanted them to think beyond the box. Our goal was to find the best people to solve the problem at hand—not make it easier for someone to get a job.

This book is designed to help you self-assess and potentially change what you believe and how you behave as a way to uncover your own innovator's spirit—or not. Think about this book like an interview. On the following pages, I'll pose more of these questions to help you on your own journey of discovery. My hope is that you'll be able to find where you are on your journey of innovation—or if you even want to pursue that journey in the first place.

In the chapters that follow, I'll discuss the fundamental concepts at the core of this book: what innovation is and what it means to lead it. I'll also talk about how innovation starts with you. It is a truly personal endeavor, and there is a specific mindset great innovators embrace on their journey of discovery.

With our foundation in place, I'll show you how innovators work from the outside in to determine what problems need to be solved—looking beyond the box. I'll also discuss how listening to customers can help (or hurt) you in getting there. The point being that sometimes the best way to innovate is to do something someone says can't be done. Finally, I'll show you how innovators lead the way in overcoming the kinds of barriers that exist in many organizations and trip most people up from ever truly innovating—such as waiting for perfection, relying on best practices, avoiding risk, and not focusing their minds.

Before you move on to the chapters that follow, consider a piece of advice: If you choose to embark on your own journey to uncover your innovator's spirit, to discover what it means to lead innovation, you will run into obstacles. Leadership is hard. You will get stuck. Don't give up. I am living proof that life will present you with another opportunity to shed the burdens that bury your innovator's spirit. All you need is the desire to keep pushing the boundaries of what those around you believe is possible. You need to look beyond the fear that you might somehow fail, because you will. It is what you learn from those failures that matters. When you can do this, your innovator's spirit will thrive.

And when you have the innovator's spirit, anything is possible.

CHAPTER ONE

Solve Problems That Create Value

"Every once in a while, a new technology, an old problem, and a big idea turn into an innovation."

—Dean Kamen

YOU'VE DECIDED YOU WANT TO uncover your innovator's spirit. That's the first step. However, before you start on this journey, we need to get calibrated on what innovation really means. It may not be what you think.

For example, how would you react if I told you that Apple, the company that brought us the Macintosh, the iPod, the iPad, and the iPhone—all of which I own—isn't innovative? Does that sound like blasphemy? Aren't Apple and innovation synonymous? At one time they were. But not anymore.

Let me explain.

I interviewed hundreds of people in my time at Cree who thought they wanted to join our company because we were considered a cutting-edge and innovative organization. I would often ask them, "Why are you interested in innovation?" The answers often included wanting to be a part of something new and exciting. While that is certainly part of the innovation experience, I also knew that there was a fair amount of pain and suffering that went along with the fun parts.

But rather than throwing cold water on the conversation right off the bat, I'd take a step back. We needed to make sure we were talking about the same thing. So I would ask the person, "What is innovation?"

What I've found in asking this question not only in interviews, but also at social functions (yeah, I'm *that* guy) and in classrooms, is that you get a wide range of answers, and many times people use the words invention and innovation interchangeably. But there's a world of difference between the two concepts—and it's critical to understand that difference if you want to uncover your innovator's spirit.

An invention, by definition, is something new—something that's never been seen before. An innovation, on the other hand, especially a disruptive one, is something new that also creates enormous value by addressing an important problem. In other words, inventions are rather common and can often collect dust while innovations change the world. Why is this distinction important to make? Because inventing something is relatively easy compared to what it takes to solve a problem and create real value.

Which brings me back to Apple—which was once perhaps the

most innovative company in the world. It's breathtaking to consider the impact that introducing the first iPhone had—and how many industries it disrupted overnight. It also changed people's lives because it solved a problem they didn't even know they had: to be connected anytime and anywhere to a handheld computer. But Apple doesn't innovate anymore. They only invent.

Around the time I was writing this book, my wife and I were talking about what I might get her as a birthday gift. I noticed that her iPhone was at least five years old. I figured that she would love one of the newer models. But when I brought up the idea, she wasn't really interested.

"Why don't you want a new phone?" I asked her.

"I just don't see any real benefit to getting a new one," she told me. "The new features like facial recognition just don't matter to me."

The thing that finally convinced her to get the upgrade was that her old phone didn't last as long on a charge anymore. The newer model would have a longer-lasting battery.

This is exactly Apple's problem in a nutshell. There's a reason that the company's sales have plateaued after a decade of incredible growth: The iPhone is no longer innovative. While market saturation has partially contributed to this trend, I believe the main reason is that Apple has become focused on inventing new features that clearly don't deliver the same value or solve problems in a way that motivates consumers to upgrade their phones. They've lost their innovator's spirit.

THE WAR OF THE CURRENTS

I was speaking to a group of college students several years ago describing the approach to innovation that we took at Cree and I explained that Thomas Edison was one of our role models. Upon hearing my reference to Edison, a young man in the audience shot up his hand in protest and proceeded to tell me that Nikola Tesla was the real innovator, because all Edison did was put his name on other people's ideas and commercialize them. It was an interesting perspective—maybe one that you share. Edison and Tesla each have hundreds of patents—thousands, in the case of Edison—registered in their names around the world. Tesla was certainly a visionary, and it is true that Edison was not a lone genius; he did work with a team of engineers. I was taken aback by this student's challenge. Was he right? But then I realized that this student was confusing the distinction between invention and innovation. Both Edison and Tesla were obviously incredibly talented inventors, but it made me want to look a little closer to understand who was the true innovator.

One of the areas that their work overlapped was in the field of electricity. In the 1880s, there was even a so-called War of the Currents as Tesla, the inventor of alternating current (AC), and Edison, who created direct current (DC) electric power, vied to see who could power the 1893 World's Fair in Chicago and, ultimately, the world itself.[1] Edison and Tesla, via the industrialist George Westinghouse, who had licensed Tesla's technology, submitted bids to see who could showcase their technology not just to the attendees of the fair, but to the rest of the world.

When the bids from the two parties were assessed, Westinghouse, using Tesla's alternating current, was the clear winner. Not only had Westinghouse's bid come in lower than Edison's, the technology also had the advantage of using fewer transformers since they could send electricity farther along transmission lines than the lower-voltage DC technology.

Thanks to this high-profile victory, AC power would soon

become the standard that continues to power much of the world's electrical grid to this very day. (It should be noted that DC power, which is used by computers and electric vehicles, is making a bit of a comeback. It's also a bit curious that the largest electric vehicle company, which is based on DC power, would be named after the inventor of AC technology. But why let facts get in the way of a good marketing story?)

So, based on this story, who was the true innovator: Tesla or Edison? It may seem obvious that it was Tesla. But the real answer is that in the case of AC versus DC power, neither Tesla nor Edison was the real innovator—it was Westinghouse. He was the one who saw the potential of the invention and used it to create real value for people by cost-effectively bringing electricity into their homes.

But you need to look further back in time to realize that Westinghouse's innovation, or even Tesla's invention, would not have been relevant without an earlier innovation by Edison: the light bulb. The light bulb was the "killer app" of its time and electricity was just the platform.

THE INNOVATOR OF MENLO PARK

When you look at the list of Edison's inventions—which ranged from the phonograph and cinema projector to an iron ore separator and a cement maker—the one that really helped him make his mark as an innovator was the incandescent light bulb. What's interesting is that Edison didn't actually invent the first light bulb: It had been originally patented in England in 1841. But it was far from a practical lighting solution—just about every home at the time used candles, oil, or gas. Edison wanted to find a way to make a light bulb that was both affordable and could remain lit for hours.

While he had already earned the nickname "The Wizard of Menlo Park," named for the New Jersey town he lived in, Edison entered a race in 1878 with some twenty other inventors to come up with a better bulb, which meant a commercially practical bulb.

What made Edison an innovator and not just an inventor was that he was always thinking about the market for his products even as he continued his work to perfect them. It was never good enough for Edison to simply create something new; he wanted to ensure that there would also be a customer who valued it. As he once said: "Anything that won't sell, I don't want to invent. Its sale is proof of utility, and utility is success."[2]

So even as he and his twenty-person team, whom he called "muckers," worked to crack the code of perfecting a workable filament for their light bulb, he was already thinking about how he would announce his breakthrough to the world. Rather than toil away in solitude, the thirty-one-year-old Edison created the Edison Electric Light Company to bring investors into his project. His pitch wasn't that he was just creating a better light bulb, but that he was really creating a new lighting "system" that would soon electrify entire towns.

In October 1878, Edison and his team finally struck upon their winning solution—a carbon filament that could burn from thirteen to forty hours at a time.[3] It had taken more than twelve hundred experiments, and $40,000, to find a workable solution.[4] But that was nothing new to Edison, who once reportedly said: "I was always afraid of things that worked the first time."[5]

That would prove to be just an opening act. On December 21, 1879, Edison ran full-page ads in the New York City newspapers announcing his "triumph in electric illumination" as well as the news that he would unveil his new creation on New Year's Eve.

The news spread and when the big day arrived, thousands of people boarded special trains to make the twenty-mile trip to Menlo Park from New York. When they arrived at Edison's campus, many wearing their very finest formal evening wear, they were dazzled as several bulbs blazed atop wooden poles lining the roadway to Edison's lab. As they entered the room, twenty-five blazing electric bulbs illuminated the room. The spectators were among the first people in the world to see the soft glow of incandescent light.[6] One attendee even called out to Edison, asking him: "How did you get that red-hot hairpin into that bottle?" There were then gasps when Edison, wearing a dirty lab coat, demonstrated how the bulbs could remain lit even when submerged in water. People began begging Edison to allow them to buy bulbs for themselves—even if they had no way yet to power them. Edison had identified a problem that customers valued.

What was clear, though, was that Edison's vision of combining the light bulb with a distribution system that could power entire nations would soon become a reality. It would be just three years later that Edison would open the first commercial power station in the nation on Pearl Street in New York City. As the share prices of the Brooklyn Gaslight Company began to collapse, shareholders in the Edison Electric Light Company saw the value of their investment skyrocket from $100 a share to more than $4,500 a share.[7,8] The idea that electricity could be provided as a utility was now possible.

BENEFITS DRIVE INNOVATION—NOT FEATURES

One of the key takeaways from the Edison and Tesla story is that just because you invent something amazing, that doesn't guarantee in any way that it will become an innovation. I know because I've been there.

When we were developing a new product, our goal was to create an innovation. But that's far easier said than done. One of the ways I would try to focus our team on this concept was to ask: "What are the benefits?" Invariably, the team would rattle off a list of features that the new product had. Our Lighting team would often tell me that it was more efficient or had better light quality. Our LED business would tout that the new product was brighter than the previous version. The team would be proud of their answers until I said something like "Those are great features, but what are the benefits?" It would generally take a minute or so for someone to recognize that they had fallen into the trap that most inventors face. Inventors see the features; they see what is new. But customers don't pay for features; they pay for benefits. It's those benefits that create the value and ultimately define an innovation.

In the case of our lighting business, the benefits were that you could see better and the lights saved you money. For LEDs, the benefit of brighter LEDs was that they used less power, which enabled battery-based products to run longer. Innovators see benefits and find ways to help the customer see them as well. Edison, by lighting up the night on New Year's Eve in Menlo Park, let his future customers see the benefit of electricity in action.

While I understand that benefits drive innovation, I'm also an engineer at heart. I enjoy developing new technology and I am not immune from falling into the features trap. A lesson I learned on my own journey to uncover my innovator's spirit involved a contract Cree signed to provide a super-high-end computer monitor to a major computer manufacturer—one that was well known for its innovative products. This company was so secretive we were not allowed to mention it by name, so we simply referred to it as the "fruit company." It wanted us to build an LED-powered backlight for a monitor that could display color schemes that would exactly mimic whatever the final use would be. If you needed to see what a four-color magazine advertisement looked like, for instance, the backlight would adjust for printing. If you wanted to see what the color looked like on a documentary film you were making, the backlight would adjust to film so the monitor could get the color just right. Whatever the medium, this monitor needed to deliver. In short, the client wanted the greatest monitor the world had ever seen.

It was exactly the kind of challenge we relished tackling: making something that seemed impossible a reality. The client had a difficult problem and was asking us to help solve it. Unfortunately, we got caught up in the features the fruit company was asking for instead of looking beyond its requests and resolving the key innovation questions we had left unanswered. If we solved this problem, would the benefit create real value for their customer? And if so, how much value would it create?

Even though we hadn't answered those questions, we embarked on the project anyway. The fruit company was considered the most innovative company in the world at that time, so we figured that they must know what they're doing. We called our new backlight system "ColorWave." And it was glorious. I had one of the test monitors on my desk, and photos looked better on that screen than they ever could on any piece of paper. I had no doubt it was the world's best computer monitor. It was an incredible piece of technology. It had all the features the client demanded. And it was a failure. Why? Because it was too expensive. The benefits didn't create enough value for the customer to justify the cost.

The reason the product became so expensive was that our client, the unnamed fruit company, kept raising the technical requirements as we were developing the backlight for the monitor. One of the primary constraints was that the monitor couldn't have any vent holes to help cool the unit—which meant that we had to more than double the number of LEDs to reduce the power levels so we could rely on the conduction of heat through the chassis to keep the system cool. That increased the cost exponentially. Whenever we pushed back on the client and let them know the cost was skyrocketing, they told us not to worry; they had customers who would pay for these features. "OK," we said, "we trust you," and it came back to bite us. We were skeptical all along, but we wanted to believe the client. We were having so much fun inventing a great piece of technology that we lost focus on the need to create value.

As we moved ColorWave into production and sent our first shipment to the client, we received a frantic call from them: "Stop the orders. We want to cancel the contract." I was completely taken aback. Cancel the contract? Why? Apparently, they had figured out what we had been questioning all along: The monitors were too expensive—the price didn't justify the benefit. I was furious, but rather than lose future business with the fruit company, we scrapped the entire project—including the manufacturing equipment and existing inventory. It really was an incredible product (I wish I had kept mine), but it failed a critical test every innovator should consider: Does it solve a problem the customer wants solved (in this case it did), and do the benefits create enough value to justify the cost (in this case it didn't)? If both aren't true, it's not an innovation—it's just another cool invention that will end up on the shelf.

BEYOND PRODUCTS AND TECHNOLOGY

If you search online for terms like "greatest innovators of all time," one of the names you'll likely see near the top is Benjamin Franklin, one of the Founding Fathers of the United States. He was a gifted diplomat, journalist, and inventor. Everyone learns in school about how it was he who, by tying a metal key to a kite and flying it into a thunderstorm, discovered electricity—something that would later fuel Tesla and Edison. Franklin was a brilliant man. But what if I told you that the greatest innovator in our country's history may have been George Washington?

Innovation doesn't just apply to electricity, or lighting, or other technical solutions. It applies to all aspects of our lives. Consider the one innovation that the United States is known for the world over. It is not a product per se, but a way of thinking. A new way to organize and govern society: representative democracy.

Not long ago I visited the city of Philadelphia. I had some time to kill, so I waited in line for a tour with John, a National Park Service guide, of the buildings where America's Founding Fathers sat down to hammer out the documents that shaped a new country and created a new type of government.

John was amazing. He was full of energy and knowledge, and he was able to tell the story in a way that it felt like we were actually there, listening to the debate about how our new government should work. He helped open my eyes to the truly astounding events that had taken place in the City of Brotherly Love. I learned that the ideas for the system of government the U.S. Constitution put in place were developed many centuries earlier by the Greeks and Romans, among others, and more recently in the Magna Carta from England. But it was the men who met in Philadelphia in the summer of 1776 to draft the Declaration of Independence, and then again in the summer of 1787 to draft the Constitution, who turned those ideas into a world-changing innovation. It was people like Franklin, Thomas Jefferson, James Madison, John Adams, and Alexander Hamilton who worked together to craft the documents that led to a new form of government run by the people, for the people. It was a marvelous invention—and it all could have shriveled away if not for Washington.

John explained that while Washington led the revolutionary forces to victory over the British during the war, he had retreated to his home at Mount Vernon in Virginia soon afterward. He figured his duty to the nation was done. But members of the first Constitutional Convention recognized that they needed Washington to serve in the role as the country's first president: He alone was the one who could shoulder the burden of leading the fledgling country in its first steps. So when the members of the Electoral College nominated Washington for the role—and voted unanimously for him—he reluctantly mounted his horse and rode to serve his country once again.

It's important to remember how unbelievably popular Washington was at the time. Some politicians even tried to make his ascension to the presidency permanent—they wanted to make him a king— an "American Caesar."[9] But Washington wasn't interested; he knew that was the idea they had fought against. And while he reluctantly served a second term in office to try and keep the nation together, he did step down after serving for eight years as president—setting a precedent that other presidents would follow for another eighty-four years. John told us that, while we might not realize it, when Washington ceded the presidency to his successor, John Adams, he changed the world. A peaceful transfer of power from one leader to the next had occurred—something that didn't happen in other countries around the world at the time. Even King George III of England, upon hearing the news that Washington was abdicating the presidency, said: "If he does that, he will be the greatest man in the world."[10]

There's no doubt Washington could have remained in power—perhaps even if the voters had turned against him. In voluntarily giving up his role, he led the way in preserving the innovative, and still fragile, system of government the founders had created that would last for 250 years and counting. As Joseph Ellis, the author of *Founding Brothers*, among other books, writes about Washington: "He became the supreme example of the leader who could be trusted with power because he was ready to give it up."[11] He was always someone who led by example. That's how you lead innovation.

CHAPTER ONE RECAP

Belief: You have to go beyond the invention.

Behavior: Solve problems that create value.

KEY INSIGHTS

Innovation defined. An innovation is something new that also creates enormous value by addressing an important problem. If both aren't true, it's just an invention.

Benefits, not features. Inventors like features, but customers pay for benefits. It's the benefits that define an innovation.

Innovation applies to everything. Innovation isn't just about products or other technical solutions—it has the power to affect all aspects of our lives.

CHAPTER TWO

Lead, Don't Manage

"Management is about persuading people to do things they do not want to do, while leadership is about inspiring people to do things they never thought they could."

—Steve Jobs

EARLY ON IN MY TENURE as CEO at Cree, I had the honor to be the commencement speaker for an executive master of business administration program at a North Carolina university. I have to admit this was both pretty cool and a little nerve-racking. I was an engineer without an MBA. What unique insight and wisdom could I share that would inspire them? I focused on providing a real-world perspective that would be new, something that hadn't been taught in business school. I'm sure they were surprised when I opened my remarks by explaining that at Cree, we had an unwritten rule against hiring anyone with an MBA degree (this would change as the company evolved). I thought it was a pretty clever insight, something to get their attention. The reaction from the faces in the crowd was one of confusion, wondering if I was joking. As it became clear that I was serious, it felt like I could hear a groan from the group that had invited me. Was it awkward? Not for me, but I'm sure it was for many in the room that day.

You're probably saying, "Hold on, you refused to hire MBAs for a growing company? Uh, isn't that when you're supposed to hire them? Aren't they the ones who invested in an education that taught them management disciplines like operations, human resources, and finance? Aren't those the areas of expertise you need to run a company?" The answer is . . . not really! Not if your goal is to innovate. That was the point of my talk that day. Having management skills and training is great, but you don't *manage* innovation, you *lead* it. If the goal was innovation, those newly developed MBA skills weren't the right tools for the job. I wasn't trying to frustrate them that day; I was challenging them. I wanted them to look beyond those three letters they could now put after their name, to look beyond what they had learned and ask themselves if they wanted to do something bigger, if they wanted to be innovative, if they wanted to be leaders.

If I asked you to tell me the difference between managing and leading, what would you say? It's been my experience that people use these terms interchangeably. But leadership and management are completely different concepts. While they might not be diametrically opposed, the behaviors often are. In the context of innovation, it's like comparing apples and spinach, and to an innovator, management is the spinach.

Leadership is the art of motivating a group of people to work toward achieving a possible future reality. Leaders get people to take risks in an attempt to overcome a challenge or achieve something new and better. Success is measured by what the team learns while striving for the larger goal.

Management, on the other hand, is the process of getting people to follow rules or procedures to achieve defined objectives. Managers use these practices to reduce risk and deliver predictable outcomes. Success is measured by how well each person does their job, follows the process, and delivers the expected result.

Peter Drucker, who shaped much of the thinking about the modern business corporation, distinguished the difference this way: "Management is doing things right; leadership is doing the right things."[1]

If you want to tap into your innovator's spirit, you'll need to think about how your existing beliefs and behaviors affect how you think and work—especially as they relate to how you embrace conventional wisdom and so-called management best practices.

Think about it. Management is designed to produce an expected result and deliver more of the same. This approach runs completely counter to creating something new, something that's never been done before. Management is specifically designed to prevent the behaviors that enable innovation.

Leading innovation, on the other hand, means believing in an idea or agreeing to pursue a goal without knowing exactly how to reach the destination. Leadership is getting people to work together to do things that haven't been done before—or to deploy old ideas in new ways—in pursuit of something bigger than themselves.

Make no mistake, the world needs both effective managers as well as leaders of innovation. But, ultimately, you have to understand your strategy and decide which approach is best to drive the desired outcome, because the two approaches are inherently in conflict. I'm not suggesting that one is better than the other. The reason we didn't hire MBAs at Cree early on was because we needed leaders who were singularly focused on finding new ways to solve problems, not people who were trying to put their hard-earned *management* skills to work.

WHY THE DISTINCTION MATTERS

Look at the lists of the best-managed companies and compare them to the lists of the most innovative companies—there's almost never any overlap. Why? The answer is quite simple. The criteria that define success on these two lists are different. Management is about controlling resources to optimize predictable outcomes, while leadership is about inspiring resources to create new and unpredictable outcomes. How does a system designed to produce predictable outcomes deliver something new and innovative? It doesn't. By definition, the best-managed companies simply cannot innovate. Just think about our story of Apple and how it has lost its innovative spirit. As the company has become phenomenal at managing the business to maximize profits, it has stopped creating innovative products.

In the early days of Cree, we wanted to compete with the big companies in our industry. This might seem counterintuitive—they had great brands, established channels, healthy balance sheets, and many more resources available to develop new technology than we could even imagine. Were we crazy? A little, but we were probably more naïve than anything. Although it seemed like they had it all, what we discovered was that, despite their size, scale, and resources, those companies were painfully slow to develop new technology. We realized that many of the management processes and practices used to run larger companies actually impede innovation.

We were small, fast, flexible, and under-resourced. They had experts who knew how things were supposed to work, who knew what wasn't possible. We were a young, inexperienced group of innovators who believed anything was possible. It really felt that way. As one of the founders would say, we also had ignorance on our side. If we had really known what it was going to take, I'm not sure anyone would have started down this path. But we didn't know; our naïveté was our advantage. So we did what leaders do—we pursued what others thought wasn't possible. Our lack of resources and experience and our belief that we had nothing to lose became an advantage. You've heard the phrase that "necessity is the mother of invention"? Well, it's also the mother of innovation. We didn't know how we were going to do it, but we just knew or, more important, *believed* it could be done. This was our opportunity to develop new technology that would disrupt their businesses and maybe even change the world. This probably sounds more like faith or religion than a well-defined business process. That's because it is! Innovation is a *mindset*, not a process. We believed we were leaders, so we acted like leaders. This approach was our competitive advantage.

I saw the other side of this issue firsthand early in my career at Hewlett-Packard (HP). I remember working with a colleague on a strategy presentation to a group of senior managers in our division. We were concerned that we were falling behind our competitors and missing some important market trends. Our goal was to show the managers the problems we saw and encourage them to consider some new ideas to transform our business and regain our competitive edge. We did plenty of research and even found sources from other industries to bolster our argument. We wanted this committee to see that we needed to think differently. That we needed to lead. But they didn't see a problem. They believed things were just fine. They were managers.

We were hitting our quarterly goals and people were getting their bonuses. The current approach was working. Why mess with success? But we weren't talking about what we had done. We were focused on what we could see coming. We were even so bold as to tell these senior managers, who were several levels above us, not to believe what they were being told by the people who reported to them. We wanted to really shake things up, so at the end of our presentation, we showed a slide that said "Don't believe them"—an idea borrowed from Donald Petersen's book, *A Better Idea,* about his tenure leading Ford Motor Company through its own difficult transformation. We were begging our managers to lead. Was it intimidating to challenge them? A little, but we were committed to trying to do what we believed was the right thing. I remember feeling like we had nothing to lose.

After our presentation, one of the senior managers looked at us and said, "We really appreciate your comments, but you shouldn't worry so much. There have been many competitors over the last twenty years, but we're still here and most of them are gone. Our approach has made us successful and it will keep making us successful." Wow. I think he was trying to make us feel good, but it had the opposite effect. I was dismayed. Didn't they hear anything we said? In hindsight, I know they heard us, but they were doing what they'd been trained to do—they were managing. While I stayed at HP for another couple of years, it was never the same. Our division fell behind in the market and was eventually sold to another company. Management thinking combined with a bit of arrogance led to its demise.

My breaking point came the day I was appointed to a committee that was assigned the task of tackling variances we were experiencing in our budgeting process. As the discussion with the other committee members progressed, it became clear I had entered the Twilight Zone. Rather than discussing the reasons the variances were occurring—or even suggesting ways to avoid them in the future—my colleagues were completely focused on understanding how they could better forecast how many mistakes would occur the next month. I couldn't believe it. They were trying to create a better process to manage a process that was already flawed. They wanted to predict mistakes rather than tackling the real problems and finding ways to innovate around them. They had become sucked into the bureaucracy and management thinking rather than chasing after what really mattered. I realized they were focused on the wrong problem, so I excused myself and never went back to another one of those meetings. HP was caught in the management trap and I knew I needed to do something different.

AVOIDING THE MANAGEMENT TRAP

We are the sum of our experiences—which includes our family lives, our time at school, and our tenures at work. And most of us have been taught to follow a set of rules most of our lives—to color inside the lines, if you will.

It makes sense as a top-down way to control chaos and variability while minimizing risk. Parents and teachers don't necessarily want children going off on their own and making their own decisions. Too messy. There's no reason for children to make the same mistake when an adult already knows the answer. Similarly, most bosses rely on standard processes that ensure everything at work is planned and measured. They want predictability, not creative thinking. Predictability is highly valued—whether in the form of a sales forecast, weekly manufacturing output report, or monthly budget—and for good reason: Making mistakes gets people fired, but hitting the numbers gets you promoted. That's why so many companies turn to automation and robots; they reduce risk and deliver predictable outcomes.

This is Management 101 behavior at work: You measure your success by how well you do your job, follow the process, and deliver the predicted result. Under-promising and over-delivering is a career advancement path. When you do that, you protect your job (avoid personal risk) and you might even get a raise. What you won't do is innovate. Ask yourself which option is better:

A. You sign up for three percent growth and deliver five percent.

B. You sign up for twenty percent growth and deliver ten percent.

In most organizations, option A is considered "better." The person who beats their forecast is considered a better manager— and they are!—even though the company would be much better off with the ten percent result. That's because the objective of a management process is to deliver a predictable result—not the *best* result. What's more important is to ask yourself what you would do in the same situation. It's really easy to look at the math and see option B is better for the company. But would you really sign up for twenty percent growth if you didn't have to? Why not take the three percent goal and beat it? Most people I've met would like to think they'd sign up for the bigger number, but in my experience most people actually sign up for the lower goal. Why take the risk? Because you rarely accomplish something great unless you set out to accomplish it in the first place. That's what leadership looks like. That's how innovation leaders act.

The more you try to make innovation a process, the less you'll innovate. When you add boundaries, structures, and rules, you kill innovation. While you may be able to generate some incremental improvements with a process, you simply cannot achieve anything akin to disruptive innovation because you have limited the kinds of outcomes you can generate. That's why organizations that have embraced best practices like total quality management or Six Sigma targeted at reducing variability find that while their quality might improve, they have also shut off the valves of creativity.

I saw this issue firsthand as we were trying to help a large global lighting company in its effort to develop an LED bulb. We were the LED component supplier, developing even brighter and more efficient LEDs. Our goal was to enable the traditional light bulb company to design an LED bulb using our LEDs that would forever relegate Thomas Edison's 130-year-old invention to the history books and museum shelves. Over the course of two years, we tried everything to make this company successful. When the lighting company struggled to meet the performance levels, we developed even brighter LEDs to help it achieve the goal. But this only made the problem worse. How? Because every time we provided a new LED, the company's process required it to start over. The company was in a constant "do loop," following its process with no way out. Its process was designed to deliver a product that would have no defects. And it worked, because the company delivered no products! We eventually gave up and developed our own LED bulb, built a factory, signed a major retail partner, and released the product across the country in less than a year. But we'll come back to that story.

LEADING IN ACTION

The pursuit of innovation starts with an idea about how to solve a problem and what success would look like. The idea is based on a combination of facts, theories, and your instincts, but it is still just an idea. You may have an estimate for how long it will take and how much it will cost—but it is only a guess. That's why I mentioned the story in the introduction and asked the question about how many barbers there are in New York City. What you are trying to do has never been done before. What you know is much less than what you don't know. That's why innovation requires leadership.

I witnessed an example of leading innovation several years ago while serving on a university board. The president had come up with an ambitious plan to build a new athletic performance and research facility on campus. He brought a unique perspective to his role as president since he had been part of a start-up earlier in his career. The facility would create much-needed space for several new sports teams, while also studying human performance by bringing several different disciplines together under one roof. It was a great concept. This facility would put the university at the forefront of a burgeoning new field of research that would help create jobs, boost the university's brand, and fill a real gap in understanding what drives human performance. But there were big costs associated with this big vision—his team estimated that the facility might cost more than $100 million—which the university couldn't afford on its own. I liked the idea, but as a board member I was worried how we would pay for it. The president's plan was to find industry partners to help share the cost.

The president had a concept, but he was betting on himself and his team to figure things out along the way. While this approach makes complete sense if you're in the business of innovation, it made many of the process-driven people within the university and on the board nervous. They wanted to know: "How exactly are we going to pull this off?" What they didn't fully understand is that the president didn't know—and didn't need to know yet—which created a lot of tension along the way.

The president knew that this is what innovation looked like. He didn't need to know exactly how everything was going to turn out; he just needed to be what I refer to as "directionally correct" (a concept I will explain further in Chapter Eleven). Part of leading innovation is testing your ideas and adjusting to new information as it comes. Not knowing exactly how it will turn out is part of doing something new. The president understood that while he owned the ultimate outcome, there were things outside his control that he would have to deal with as he and his team figured things out along the way.

As the project progressed, some things worked as expected—but many did not. It didn't matter, as they were learning new information to guide the next step. Some of the failures became more valuable than the successes. In one case, some faculty members raised a concern that the facility was too narrowly focused on elite athletes. The president used the feedback to expand the scope of which athletes the building would serve. In another case, the partners that originally committed funding to the project backed away, so the president adjusted the scale of the facility. With each change in plans, the president helped the team continue to believe they would be successful. And they were. In the end, the university succeeded in building a $25 million facility that supports cutting-edge research on athletic performance, not just for world-class athletes but for all athletes—including those with disabilities. The project was a complete success. It solved a problem and created value by the very fact that it now exists and is doing something that otherwise wouldn't have been possible.

ELIMINATING ORGANIZATIONAL BIAS

While it's easy to say the key to innovation is leadership (which it is), it's also important to understand the management bias that is built into many organizations. In the early days of Cree, management thinking was not only avoided, it was not even tolerated—especially when it got in the way of innovation. That's easy to say but hard to do. People have been trained in management thinking by the many examples that exist all around them, even if they don't realize it.

One of the things I wanted to know about people who were interviewing at Cree was whether they could operate in a leadership-driven organization. As I would often tell people, some companies are process-driven, but at Cree we're people-driven. Process is fixed and slow to change, but innovation requires speed and the ability to adapt to new information. In our people-driven approach, we gave up control and predictability and bet on our people to find a better way. That sounds nice, but it's actually quite challenging, due to the biases that most people bring with them.

For example, consider the powerful management bias that comes from something that seems innocuous: the organizational chart. To see how someone thinks, I would draw the following picture on a white board:

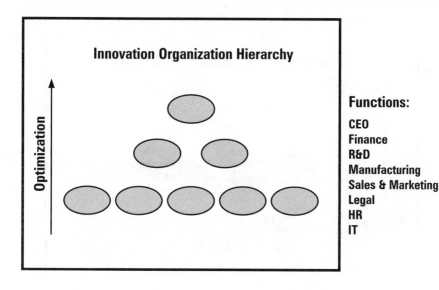

Innovation Organization Hierarchy

Optimization

Functions:

CEO
Finance
R&D
Manufacturing
Sales & Marketing
Legal
HR
IT

Then I would ask the person to fill in the chart, with the different functions of an organization. Things like finance, human resources, sales, and research and development, plus a spot for the CEO. You should try it yourself, before reading on.

The results were quite interesting and would tell me a lot about the person I was talking to. In most cases, the person would put the CEO at the top, followed by whatever function they were part of. Finance people put finance near the top. Manufacturing people would put manufacturing near the top. Sales people put sales near the top. You get the idea.

I would then ask that person to keep in mind that our primary business was innovation. Would they make any changes if they were optimizing for this? Usually they would make some changes to their original chart. Then I would show them what the actual chart looked like at Cree.

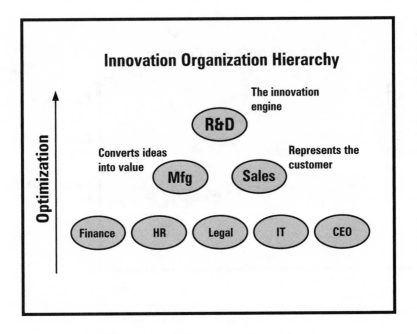

I would explain that we were in the business of innovation, and our thinking was not built around a traditional org chart. Instead, our company was optimized around the constraints that were most critical to our success. At the top was R&D, because without great new ideas that solved customer problems, our strategy would fail. I would also point out that R&D represented the innovators in all parts of the company. New ideas were welcome from any function, and the rest of the organization should ensure that they didn't do things that would de-optimize this role. In fact, we would purposely make other functions a lower priority to promote innovation. The second level was sales and marketing, which represented the customer. Our products weren't innovative without customers who valued them. The other function was operations or manufacturing, because we sold products, not ideas, and ultimately it was manufacturing that turned those ideas into something tangible that the customer would pay for.

I then explained that this chart wasn't written down, but we expected people to behave in this manner. Some people saw this and were excited to join the company. Others, like those in finance or human resources, saw this and sometimes felt that we didn't value their role. We did value their role, not because of where it fell on the org chart, but because of their ability to help us create value for our customers. If they could embrace this idea, we felt they could be effective in our leadership-driven innovation company. If they were bothered by it, it was better that they didn't join to start with.

The goal of this exercise was to be very clear in our expectations. Innovation came first, and we were committed to removing traditional organizational bias that got in the way. To reinforce this point, we didn't publish an organizational chart for many years. You knew who your boss was; what else did you need to know? Our idea was to eliminate the management bias that comes from formal structures. We wanted everyone to focus on what they could do to help us innovate, and the rest would take care of itself. It seemed very logical to us, but we had to continually manage the tension that people brought with them from traditional organizations.

This conversation was also a test of ego. We were looking for people who had enough ego to drive them to succeed. At the same time, they needed to be comfortable knowing that it wasn't about them—it was about achieving our shared goal. If the organization discussion made them uncomfortable, I was pretty sure they didn't have the balance we were looking for.

THE TENSION NEVER ENDS

The battle between leadership and management doesn't just happen at large companies. It happens every day in small companies that build their business through innovation, and then put in place management practices as they get larger. It happened to me during my sixteen years as the CEO of Cree. During this time, Cree grew from a small LED chip company with a little over $100 million in revenue into a global $1.6 billion company with three distinct business units: LEDs, Lighting, and Power & RF (radio frequency). Power & RF would later be renamed Wolfspeed.

LEDs were the largest business and provided the majority of our profits. We built the business through innovation and as it matured, the competitive landscape intensified. We adapted our approach in an effort to maintain innovation leadership, while at the same time implementing the management process necessary to operate at scale. While there was tension in this approach, we demonstrated that it was possible to find a balance, although it did reduce our ability to innovate.

Our Lighting business was built around the innovation of long-lasting LED lighting. We started the LED lighting revolution with our groundbreaking technology that saved energy, lasted longer, and saved the customer money over the life of the product. It was a truly disruptive innovation, which led to tremendous growth from $30 million to $800 million in only a few years. The growth challenged our team's ability to execute, and things started to get out of control. We struggled to hit our financial plan and customer service suffered. So we implemented numerous management processes and controls in an effort to deliver more predictable results. We tried to find the same balance that had worked in the LED business, but we went too far. The people we put in charge to manage those outcomes established rules and processes that killed our innovation engine. Everything took longer, and our new products were no longer groundbreaking. They were incremental. And the business was never the same.

This change in our beliefs and behaviors was driven by the fact that, as a public company, we were accountable to our shareholders who were focused on our quarterly numbers. I recall an investor who offered some good advice. "I tell companies that when they are generating value through innovation that they shouldn't be in a hurry to make a profit," he told me. "The moment you start to make profits, you'll be judged on that and that alone and it will force you to change your behaviors." He was right—only I didn't fully appreciate his advice at the time.

We continued to grow as a company and earn healthy profits, but we also killed the environment that made innovation thrive in our business. Managers were put in leadership roles. More processes and controls delayed the big new ideas. The environment devolved into separate groups who were focused on their individual goals, not the bigger goal. The conversations shifted from "I own it and will find a solution" to "I did my part and that's not my responsibility." We achieved many of the metrics, but we lost our ability to innovate. All was not lost, however.

At the same time, our Power & RF business continued to operate in innovation mode. The business unit was small enough to not fall under the same investor scrutiny as LEDs and Lighting. We stayed focused on driving innovation, but the results were unpredictable and sometimes frustrating. We reached a point where we had been working on the technology for twenty-five years and still hadn't created real value. I wasn't sure we'd ever get there, so we announced a plan to spin off the Power & RF business. This resulted in several companies contacting us asking to buy it outright. After almost a year of negotiations, we had a deal to sell the business to a large German semiconductor company for $800 million. A great price for such a small business. The one catch was the U.S. government had to approve the sale, since some of the technology was restricted by the government. We weren't worried, because no German company had ever been rejected. But after almost a year of working through the approval process, the unexpected happened. The deal was rejected. No reason was given; it was just rejected. Two years of effort and our $800 million deal was dead. It would turn out to be the best deal we never made.

During the two years we spent trying to spin off and then sell the business, the technology continued to improve, and the market changed. We soon found ourselves designed into several important applications, including electric vehicles. Orders started coming in and we were soon sold out and announcing a major capacity expansion. Today, the Power & RF business has become the growth engine for the entire company. The smallest business is projected, as of the writing of this book, to become the biggest business because we didn't let management processes kill the innovation.

It's also a lesson in not giving up. We invested in this technology for thirty years, thinking for most of that time the big market was just around the corner, only to give up and almost sell the business right before it was about to take off. Innovation often requires a healthy combination of patience and perseverance in the face of logic telling you it's time to move on.

IT STARTS WITH YOU

Understanding the difference between what it means to lead innovation—as opposed to manage it—is a foundational concept that the following chapters will build on. So many of us are trapped under the burden of these management principles we've been trained on our whole lives that the beliefs and behaviors that drive the innovator's spirit might seem strange or counterintuitive at first. But if you are willing to embrace a different mindset, you are already one step closer to tapping into your own innovator's spirit.

CHAPTER TWO RECAP

Belief: Leadership enables innovation; management kills innovation.

Behavior: Lead, don't manage.

KEY INSIGHTS

Innovation requires leadership. Management and leadership are completely different concepts. You need to constantly work to avoid the management trap.

Eliminate organizational bias. Organizations are inherently designed as management or control structures, which work against the leadership thinking required to do something new.

The tension never ends. Stakeholders will drive short-term thinking if you let them. It is the leader's job to keep them focused on the value in solving the big problem.

CHAPTER THREE

Embrace the Brutal Truths

"The truth is incontrovertible. Malice may attack it, ignorance may deride it, but in the end, there it is."
—**Winston Churchill**

WHAT ARE BRUTAL TRUTHS? THEY describe the style of communication that is critical to uncovering your innovator's spirit. Many people talk about the need to give direct and honest feedback, and yet what happens in practice is usually quite the opposite. Think of how many times you've sat in a meeting listening to somebody promote an idea that most in attendance knew wouldn't work. Did anyone call them out? Did anyone say, stop, we're wasting time because your idea will never work? Probably not, but it does happen. Let me tell you about my first experience with the brutal truth.

When I first joined Cree, my position was LED product manager. Over the next year or so, I was increasingly given more responsibilities—including figuring out how to buy another company in Hong Kong. After that acquisition, Neal Hunter, my boss and the CEO at the time, decided that I had earned a promotion running our newly acquired business—and a spot at the table at the weekly leadership team meetings.

I was feeling pretty good about things when I walked into my first meeting. As I took my seat at the conference table, Neal began handing out pieces of paper to everyone. As I looked at my copy, my stomach dropped. It was a photocopy of an email I had recently sent to one of our customers in Germany, which Neal had been copied on. As I glanced at what I had written, I saw my mistake: Instead of starting the note with "I'm," I had written "I." A typo. No big deal, right? We all do that. So why was everyone getting a copy of my email?

Neal kicked off the discussion by pointing to my email and saying: "I want you all to read this and ask yourselves if we can afford to be this sloppy with our customers. If we really want to make it as a company, we have to take the time to do things the right way." He then proceeded to make a comment about the "spell check generation" and our reliance on the computer to find mistakes, instead of being accountable for taking time to get it right. I think I stopped listening at some point. I just stared at my mistake that was there for all to see.

If you've ever been called out in front of your peers, you can probably imagine how I felt. Quite frankly, I was initially furious with Neal. How could he make such a big deal about a stupid typo?

I then became mad at myself. How could I have been so careless? I was totally embarrassed and wondered how I would ever earn the respect of my peers.

But by the time I walked out of that meeting an hour later, I began to understand what Neal was trying to teach me. He was introducing me to the power of facing the brutal truth. He was challenging me to do better. And he did it by cutting through the professional niceties that we're so accustomed to these days. I was the one who had to take responsibility for my mistake—and to do better going forward. That's how I would earn the respect of my peers. It was then that I truly understood why, if you want to innovate—where you solve the hard problems that create real value—you have to be willing to handle the brutal truth of the situation you find yourself in. The brutal truths lead to the facts. And the facts, good or bad, are a critical part of the learning process and knowing exactly what problems need to be solved.

Consider this statement from Guy Kawasaki, an early Apple employee: "Steve Jobs' idea of HR was to rip you in front of all your peers."[1] Kawasaki said that he lived in fear of being embarrassed in front of his peers—which became a motivating force that inspired him to do some of the best work of his career. That's the counterintuitive power of the brutal truths.

YOU ARE RESPONSIBLE FOR YOUR OWN EMOTIONAL STATE

Who is responsible for whether or not you are offended by what someone says in a conversation at work? The person making the comment or the person on the receiving end of the comment? What if I said that each person is responsible for their own emotional state? Does it make you rethink your answer? I hope it does, because this is a critical part of discovering your innovator's spirit.

How would you react if someone told you your idea was "stupid"? Does that sound unprofessional and maybe even a bit childish? Would you be offended? At Cree, the word *stupid* was a normal part of conversation—especially in the early days. Whether you were in a meeting or talking to someone one-on-one, you might hear something described as stupid if the situation called for it. Why? The word provides very clear feedback. No subtlety. No beating around the bush. No extra words to try and soften the message. Most important, it isn't personal. But how can that be? It's my belief that you have a choice—it's only personal if you choose to take it that way. If the listener assumes the person giving the feedback is talking about an idea, and not the person (which is sometimes easier said than done), it's an incredibly efficient and direct way to cut to the heart of the matter. Think about how freeing it is to know exactly what the other person thinks instead of wasting time and energy wondering what someone really meant. In my experience, many organizations spend far more time dancing around tough issues in the name of being nice or polite than they do actually working on those issues. While there are certainly lines you should never cross, such as criticizing the person instead of the idea, being brutally honest is a critical part of the innovator's feedback process. This concept wasn't something we talked about; it was a fact of everyday life that everyone accepted.

Or at least I thought everyone did until the day I was in a spirited discussion with several colleagues, which included John Edmond, one of the company founders, and Chris, a recently hired senior leader. During the debate, Chris made a suggestion—which John immediately said was stupid. I didn't even notice the comment when it was made, as we were all problem-solving in real time. After the meeting ended, Chris walked back to my office with me and asked me if I had a minute. I said sure, assuming he wanted to talk more about the topic we had been discussing. But when we sat down in my office, Chris looked across the table and said, "That was a very offensive thing to say."

I had no idea what he was referring to. I had to replay the last few minutes in my head. We had just come up with several promising ideas to solve the problem we were working on. I was feeling like we had made great progress.

"I don't understand. What was offensive?" I asked.

"John said my idea was stupid," Chris fired back, referring to a comment he had made during the meeting. It was an aha moment for me—and not the good kind. So I asked Chris, "When he made that comment, do you think John was talking about you or your idea?"

"I don't know, does it matter?" he responded.

"It matters a lot," I said. "Assume there was nothing personal about the comment—that he was only responding to your idea. Does it change your perspective? Is it still offensive?"

After a pause, Chris said, "I guess not, but it still seems harsh. Why did he say it?"

"Because your idea was, in fact, not going to work," I replied. "It was illogical given the situation. John was telling you that, in his opinion, you had a stupid idea."

I then explained to Chris that we believed in being very direct. The brutal truths were our way to inspire real honesty about a problem, which would then fuel the creativity to find a solution that would add value. I don't know how much Chris really understood that day. I was challenging a deeply held belief he had. But, over time, he was able to embrace our direct style and uncover a part of his innovator's spirit.

As I've explained this concept to many people, it has caused a lot of reaction, and not all of it positive. Some people are simply offended by the word *stupid*, which I understand. That's why I use it—to illustrate that the brutal truths can be really hard for many people to embrace. I want to be clear that the brutal truths are not about whether you should use the word *stupid*. That is simply an example from my time at Cree. The key to this concept is not the specific words you use, but your ability to be honest with yourself, your peers, and your team, and their ability to be direct with you. To make this work, you first need to establish trust among your team members. This requires both leadership skill and emotional intelligence. You must be able to give honest feedback and, more important, be willing to hear it when it is directed your way. You have to be able to separate the problem from the person, and everyone needs to agree not to take it personally—which comes down to each person realizing that they are responsible for their own mental state.

The leader plays a critical role in making this concept work. The leader must set the tone for the team to ensure that honest and direct feedback is about the ideas and not about the people. To ensure that the feedback is a two-way street. And to ensure that the brutal truths are not used as a tool by some to intimidate or quiet others.

FACING THE FACTS

Have you ever sat in a meeting whose purpose was to "brainstorm"? The goal might have been to come up with new ideas about a new product, service, or marketing campaign. Were there ground rules established at the start of the meeting? Think about what those were. In one instance early in my career, I sat down in a meeting just like this and the organizer told us there were a couple of rules we had to adhere to for the next few hours:

1. There was no such thing as a dumb idea.

2. Don't criticize someone else's idea.

You've heard these ground rules before, right? Do you agree with them? I don't. They're a fine set of guidelines if your goal is to spend a nice day together or to promote social harmony, but I can tell you from experience that they won't help you get any closer to innovating. But you don't have to trust me: There is research to back up what I learned firsthand.

The art of brainstorming as we know it was created by a man named Alex Osborn, who was a partner in the advertising agency BBDO. He not only coined the term, but he also, in his 1948 book *Your Creative Power*, brought brainstorming from the "Mad Men" of advertising into the mainstream. Criticizing other people's ideas became frowned upon in the spirit of unlocking the creative spirit. While that seems to make sense, in reality, this kind of brainstorming actually makes people *less* creative, not better at it. Multiple studies on Osborn's theories have continually debunked the notion that eliminating healthy debate is somehow productive. One of my favorites was conducted in 2003 by Charlan Nemeth, a professor of psychology at the University of California, Berkeley, and found that encouraging people to challenge each other, what she labeled the "debate condition," actually led to more good ideas. As Nemeth was quoted as saying in a *New Yorker* article titled "Groupthink: The Brainstorming Myth":[2]

While the instruction "Do not criticize" is often cited as the important instruction in brainstorming, this appears to be a counterproductive strategy. Our findings show that debate and criticism do not inhibit ideas but, rather, stimulate them relative to every other condition. There's this Pollyannaish notion that the most important thing to do when working together is [to] stay positive and get along, to not hurt anyone's feelings. Well, that's just wrong. Maybe debate is going to be less pleasant, but it will always be more productive. True creativity requires some trade-offs.

What the research reveals is that even if someone who challenges your idea is wrong, it serves as an alert mechanism for our brains, which causes us to review and reassess the situation from another point of view. "Authentic dissent can be difficult, but it's always invigorating," Nemeth said in the *New Yorker* article. "It wakes us right up." In other words, debate and facing the brutal truths help us look at the problem from a different angle—which is where innovation comes from.

At Cree, this was just a normal way of doing business. We wanted to hear the dissenting voices. (At least until we got bigger and started to lose our connection to the brutal truths.) But what I've come to realize is that many other great innovators have embraced the hard truths to push beyond their own boundary conditions. Consider the example of Andy Grove, the founder of computer chip maker Intel, who was famous for his desire to embrace the brutal truths. In fact, as an article in the online magazine *Quartz* framed it: "Grove's greatest strength as a manager may have been his ability to confront himself."[3] For example, the article points out that in the 1980s, sales of Intel's chips for minicomputers had sunk in the face of global competition. The business was still large enough that some managers might have tried to implement some incremental changes to try and save it—especially if they thought their job was on the line. But Grove wanted to look at the brutal truths. He reportedly asked one of his direct reports: "If we got kicked out and the board brought in a new CEO, what do you think he would do?" Again, Grove wasn't trying to save face in the wake of failure. He wanted to find a way to identify the real problem so he could address it. That's someone who had the innovator's spirit.

Another great case study comes from a company called Shopify. Even if you don't know what Shopify is, odds are you have bought something using it since it powers many of the e-commerce sites on the internet. A key component for how the company was able to scale from zero to today, where its revenues top $40 billion, was a dedication to the brutal truths, according to Tobi Lütke, Shopify's CEO and one of its cofounders.

Lütke says he was inspired by an early editor of the website Wikipedia named Crocker, who welcomed honest feedback from anyone as a way to make the pages he had written better. "I remember reading that Crocker said, 'I will take control of my own mental state; you cannot make me unhappy through your feedback,'" Lütke once told interviewer Tim Ferriss. Lütke loved that notion and began to apply it to his own team. "Feedback is a gift, even though that's not how most people think about it," he said. "It's not meant to hurt. It's meant to move things forward by demystifying things. I want frank feedback from everyone."[4]

Rather than waste time in meetings covering topics like the weather, Lütke wanted everyone to cut to the chase—even if that meant confronting the brutal truths. Toby Shannan, Shopify's vice president of revenue at the time, told an interviewer that Lütke never pulls his punches when it comes to getting to the facts of the moment. "Be prepared to be crushed," Shannan said. "If you can't be crushed, you don't make it on the executive team. You need a thick skin."[5]

When asked about that quote, Lütke tried to put his reputation into context: "I want our people to take their mental state in their own hands. I don't want them to have to rely on others to tell them they are doing a good job . . . I define hell as meeting the best version of yourself you could have become." In other words, if you're not willing to confront the brutal truths, how can you ever achieve your true potential?

While you and your kids might be a big fan of Pixar movies such as *Toy Story*, *A Bug's Life*, *Cars*, and *Up* like my family is, you might be surprised at how the brutal truths play a pivotal role in creating such lovable and relatable characters. Ed Catmull, one of the cofounders of Pixar, attributes the company's success to the use of candor—being forthright or frank—when working through opportunities and challenges. Pixar even had an organizational group called the "Brain Trust" whose function was to get candid feedback on whatever movies the studio happened to be working on. "A hallmark of a healthy creative culture is that its people feel free to share ideas, opinions, and criticisms," Catmull said. "Lack of candor, if unchecked, ultimately leads to dysfunctional environments."[6]

It is important to understand that being obnoxious and calling people out in meetings doesn't make you an innovator. That just makes you a jerk. Embracing the brutal truths is about the genuine pursuit of finding a better idea. I thought Kawasaki nailed this point when he told an interviewer about how he saw some people trying to emulate Steve Jobs:

The problem with Steve emulation mode is that people on the outside look at that and say well I'm going to be the next Steve Jobs, I'm not going to do market research, I'm not going to listen to anybody, I'm going to wear Levi's jeans, New Balance shoes, black mock turtlenecks, I'm going to buy a Mercedes and not register it, I'm going to drive in the carpool lane by myself, park in a handicap spot, and I'm going to be the next Steve Jobs. No you won't. You'll just be an asshole.[7]

This quote is a great reminder that while facing the facts and embracing a culture of candor is critical to innovation, how you do it also matters. You can be brutal without being an asshole—which is really important when leading a team.

THE BENEFIT OF CUTTING TO THE TRUTH

I have served as a board member for several different companies and nonprofits over the course of my career. That means that I've seen my share of executive presentations and given my share to my own board—so I'm familiar with the tension between telling the board enough and telling them too much. So what's the right balance? I've heard other CEOs describe their approach to board meetings as "tell the board as little as possible so they can perform their fiduciary role and then go home so you can get back to getting things done." It's not the most inspiring view of how things work, and you won't hear anyone publicly claiming this is their intent. But it is often what happens. Why? Even the best-intended management teams learn quickly that bad news usually causes an even worse reaction from their board. So they adapt and try to avoid bad news. This results in meetings where management presents a lot of slides in an attempt to give the board a good feeling about the business so they can keep their jobs. This issue doesn't just apply to boards and CEOs. I've seen it many times in organizations when teams present to their management.

This was not our approach at Cree. In my first years as CEO, we were probably more like other companies. Then two things happened. First, I became more confident as a leader. I realized that my hesitation in sharing problems with the board was my issue, not theirs. If I was going to lead a company based on innovation, I needed to lead the board in the same manner. Second, I had some great board members who helped me realize that the board could be an asset. As one director told me, "You need to see your board as well-paid consultants with the same overall objective as you—the company's success. You don't want or need them to do your job. But you should get your money's worth and use their expertise. To do that, they need to really understand the issues you're facing. They need to understand what keeps you up at night; they need to understand the truth about your business."

After getting that insight, I decided to start my board meetings with a discussion of what was keeping me up at night. We then asked the leaders of our different business units to share the brutal truths of their business. Rather than tell us what was going right inside the operation, we wanted our business leaders to tell us what *wasn't* going well or what was at risk of failing. We wanted them to tell us what kept them up at night and what might go wrong.

Why would we do that?

Our intent wasn't to criticize or put down the leader or the business. Just the opposite. We wanted them to lead, which starts with finding the courage to take an honest and objective look at the business. It's not always easy to do. The first time I asked a new leader to prepare their brutal truths for a board meeting, the truths weren't very brutal. But with some encouragement, and some very honest feedback from me, they quickly realized the benefit of our approach. Once the issues were out in the open, it became much easier for everyone, especially the leader, to identify the problems that needed to be fixed.

The innovation business is discovering new solutions to old problems. Our goal was to focus all of our energy on solving problems, instead of wasting time trying to pretend there weren't any. Putting the issues on the table also created alignment across the company, from the board down to the lowest levels, which raised the stakes for everyone to make sure those issues got addressed. Admitting that you don't have all the answers is often the first step to opening your mind to finding new solutions.

Most organizations don't operate this way. Openly showing your flaws is not how they teach you to climb the corporate ladder in management school. In many companies, pretending like you have all the answers is key to career success. But learning to be open to criticism and putting your brutal truths on the table for all to see can be an incredibly effective way to grow as a leader and a powerful and important tool for innovation. I'd even go so far as to say that criticism may be the true genesis for innovative thinking.

THE PRESSURE TO PLAY NICE

As Cree grew into a much larger company, it became harder to maintain our beliefs and behaviors related to facing the cold hard facts. We continued to talk about the brutal truths and present them at board meetings, but the day-to-day conversations lost their edge. Someone would say "I want to be brutally honest," instead of actually being brutally honest. When someone prefaces their comment, it is a strong indication that they're not saying what they're really thinking. When it's working correctly, they simply speak the truths as they see them. But as more people joined the company, there was a desire by many to move away from our very candid and direct communication style and focus on the positives. I was told our approach was "too harsh." Most people are uncomfortable being brutally honest.

There were moments when I was so frustrated I wanted to put everyone in a room (that would be pretty impractical with seven thousand global employees) and ask them: If innovation is about finding new solutions to problems, how are we ever going to be able to do that if we are not honestly discussing the problems? The answer, of course, is that you can't. In hindsight, I should have done it. Maybe not in one giant meeting, but there were ways for me to make my point. The brutal truth is that I stopped fighting the battle under the guise that I tried and assumed there was nothing I could do to stop the trend. But that was a cop-out. I could have done something. I should have done something. And I will do something the next time.

As we were growing the company really fast, sometimes fifty percent in a single year, we were hiring people at an almost equally fast rate. At one point our head of human resources came to my office and said, "We talk about the Cree way of doing things, but half of our employees have worked here less than two years." As a result, not only did they not fully understand our unique approach to things like the brutal truths, but they were also still carrying around beliefs and behaviors from their previous jobs. The direct style of communication that had made us so successful started to be replaced with lots of meetings where most people didn't say what they were thinking. As a result, they didn't decide much of anything.

I began focusing on trying to understand what people's beliefs were before they joined our team, especially those who were going to be expected to lead. I wanted to know how big a gap there was coming in. I would often ask: "Describe some examples of building consensus in your current job. Do you consider yourself good at building consensus? How does consensus benefit the organization?" After listening to their answers, I would come back with "What is the difference between getting consensus and getting buy-in? Which is more valuable in the pursuit of innovation?" Many people didn't appreciate the distinction, so I would explain that consensus relies on everyone agreeing, which usually eliminates the most risky, interesting, and potentially most valuable ideas. Buy-in simply requires the leader to make the best decision for the team and then gain support to pursue the idea. It's not about agreement. I would then ask: "What is your reaction to my belief that consensus building is completely counter to successful innovation?" This always led to an interesting discussion, where my point ultimately was to explain that we needed to be direct and brutally honest about what we thought. We didn't want consensus because it doesn't lead to the type of breakthrough thinking we needed to be successful.

Consider a story about Alfred P. Sloan, one of the founders of General Motors, who believed that complete agreement meant they were not pushing hard enough for the best ideas. One time when he and his management team met to discuss an important decision, Sloan decided to end the meeting by asking: "Gentlemen, I take it we are all in complete agreement on the decision here?" He then waited and watched as each person on the team gave their approval for the new plan. He then threw them a curveball by saying: "Then,

I propose we postpone further discussion of this matter until our next meeting to give ourselves time to develop disagreement and perhaps gain some understanding of what this decision is about."[8]

The pressure to be nice often came to light in the performance review process. I remember when a manager came by my office because they wanted to fire an employee. I was familiar with the employee's poor performance but told the manager it was their decision. So they left and proceeded to start the process. But early the next morning, I got a call from a member of our legal team. She asked if I had read the annual performance reviews for the employee the manager wanted to fire. I said that I hadn't but that I would check them out. You know what I found? When I read through those reviews, this employee sounded like a star—someone who had repeatedly met or exceeded expectations. Was this really the same person I saw in action? The one with a number of performance issues? The problem, it turned out, was that the employee's manager had never been willing to confront the employee with the brutal truths. Not in person and not in their performance reviews. It was as if the manager was trying to help this employee avoid the ugly truth of their performance at work. But who gained from that? Not the employee, and certainly not the company. In the end, I insisted that the manager take the time to explain the performance gaps to the employee. While the employee was disappointed, once they saw past their shock and could clearly see the reality of the situation, they understood why they were being fired.

I was somewhat infamous for my brutal honesty during performance reviews of my team. My philosophy developed during my early days at Hewlett-Packard. I remember sitting down with my boss, Aneta, during my first review. She was a great boss who really cared about developing her people. She was smiling as she walked me through the review and discussed the different performance areas. She told me I was doing a great job and exceeding expectations in all areas. I could tell it made her happy to provide such positive feedback. After she finished with her comments, she asked me for my feedback. How would you respond in this situation? Would you thank your boss and walk away feeling good about what you accomplished? I think many people would. But that's not what happened in this case. I just couldn't do it. I looked at Aneta and said: "You told me all the things I'm doing well. I appreciate that, but my goal is to do more, take on more responsibility, make a bigger impact in the company. I really want to know what I need to do better to accomplish that."

You may be thinking that I was pretty ungrateful at that moment. While that may be true, it wasn't the point. The nice feedback served no useful purpose in my pursuit of getting better—and getting better was always my goal. That's why I embraced that approach when it came time for me to review other people. Members of my team occasionally complained that I only focused on the negative aspects during those reviews, but they eventually realized that my goal was to focus the entire conversation on getting better. I believed everyone could get better. They just needed to want it and be willing to work for it. It was also important for the company. We were growing really fast and if my team was going to be part of our future, they had to grow their own abilities just as fast to keep up. We had to focus on the things that would make them successful in the next year—not the previous year. Was I too brutal? For some, yes. But for most of our team, the things they did to embrace the critical feedback and grow as leaders are what ultimately made us successful.

COACHING SOMEONE TO EMBRACE THE BRUTAL TRUTH

When I talk with people about the brutal truths, their initial reaction is usually quite positive. It seems like a great idea—until they have to do it or hear it from someone else. That is when they realize that they're not sure how to actually implement this idea. I have had the opportunity to coach many people over the years and have tried plenty of things that didn't work exactly as intended. Ultimately, I have refined my approach to the following five key ideas:

1. ESTABLISH THE BELIEF THAT IT'S NOT PERSONAL

Everyone is accountable for their own mental state. No exceptions. Nobody on the team is allowed to opt out. If you're not willing to accept this premise, you can't be on the team. It's the listener's job to hear the feedback in the appropriate context. This is easy to say and very hard for most people to do. Before you ever need to have a conversation about a brutal truth, you need to create a foundation for embracing this idea and building trust among the team. In the heat of the moment, people will naturally react based on their core beliefs, so you have to work to create this belief before the moment requires it.

2. SHOW THE PROBLEM IN AN EXAMPLE OF YOURSELF

You need the other person to lower their defense mechanisms, so they can see the problem. One of the most effective ways I found to do this is by showing the person the problem by using an example about myself. Make it about you, not them. Share an example of where you've had a similar challenge. If a person needs to communicate better with their peers, give them an example of when you struggled with the issue yourself and how it caused a problem for others. Let the person see the problem instead of the person. By doing this, you change the context of the conversation in a way that allows the other person to more quickly see the truth of the situation. Your willingness to admit you had the same struggle also makes your feedback far more relevant and relatable.

3. FOCUS ON WHAT YOU WOULD DO DIFFERENTLY THE NEXT TIME

The past is the past. While most people spend their time fixated on what went wrong and who was to blame, it really doesn't matter. The only thing that matters is whether or not the leader understands what they would do differently the next time. I would often set this up by saying something like "I want to spend one minute understanding what went wrong. Then, I want to spend the rest of our time discussing what you learned and what you would do differently the next time to get a different result." I've found that when you shift the context this way, people tend to be much more honest about a situation. It also allows you to focus on the different behaviors they could engage in to achieve the more optimal outcomes. You avoid setting off their defense mechanisms and get to see the problem from a different angle.

4. ACCEPT RESPONSIBILITY

It is critical to avoid playing the blame game. I can't tell you how many situations I have been in as a leader or, quite frankly, as a parent, when in asking someone what went wrong, their immediate instinct is to blame someone else. It's someone else's fault! This is a natural reaction but blaming someone else is not what leaders do. When something goes wrong, a leader should never point the finger anywhere other than at the mirror. The working assumption at Cree was that if something went wrong, it meant that the leader should have done something different—not that someone on the frontlines screwed up. If I asked someone what went wrong and they immediately blamed someone else, I would say, "Time out. Do you think they did something intentionally wrong? Or did you not communicate it correctly to them? What could you have done differently? If you want to be the leader, then you have to be accountable for yourself and your team."

5. TRUST BUT VERIFY

Trust but verify is often the most important teaching technique when helping someone to embrace a difficult reality. When you have a conversation about a brutal truth, the other person may accept the feedback, but that is not the same as being able to make the necessary changes. Think about it: They acted the way they did for a reason. The brutal truth may have gotten their attention, but behavior change is usually slow and takes practice and a strong desire. As the leader, you can't just provide the feedback and then hope that everything works out. It is your job to check in and make sure they're making progress, sometimes directly and other times by observing the team. There is incredible power in asking the team how everything is going and then listening to the kinds of answers you get back. Notice I didn't say micromanage the situation by telling people what to do. The goal is to check in and help reinforce the beliefs and behaviors you want from your team.

Embracing the brutal truths is only the next step in tapping into your innovator's spirit. Once you've learned to hear the truth and see the problem that needs to be addressed, the challenge shifts to your willingness to do what it takes to get to the goal—your will to win.

CHAPTER THREE RECAP

Belief: You are responsible for your own mental state.

Behavior: Embrace the brutal truths.

KEY INSIGHTS

Start with the truth. Innovation requires continuous direct and honest feedback. The facts, whether good or bad, are the first step.

Challenge one another. Using debate to face the brutal truths fully engages our minds to look at problems from different angles to find the most creative solutions.

Don't settle for harmony. There is tremendous pressure to play nice and avoid difficult people and situations. But you can't stop being brutally honest, because you will lose part of your innovator's spirit.

CHAPTER FOUR

Find a Way to Win

"The will to win, the desire to succeed, the urge to reach your full potential . . . these are the keys that will unlock the door to personal excellence."
—Confucius

INNOVATORS LOVE TO COMPETE. THEY have what I call "a will to win"—to reach a goal other people think can't be reached. They believe there is always a way to achieve the goal if they're willing to work hard enough to get there. The innovators I worked with didn't avoid unexpected challenges; they sought them out and were motivated to beat them. Why? In part, because they were drawn to the feeling of joy that came from solving a difficult problem. They also relished the challenge of competition—to do whatever it took to reach the goal. In the end, our success at Cree came down to a group of people who were committed to finding a way to win.

How do you react when something doesn't go your way? If you're playing a game—maybe cards, a board game, or a video game—how do you react when you lose? How does that make you feel? What do you do next? Do you get frustrated and walk away? Or are you inspired to try again and find a better way to play? How you answer these questions can tell you a lot about your will to win—and whether or not you've uncovered your innovator's spirit.

When you're innovating, it's inevitable that you'll run into dead ends and uncover new information that can cause you to change your mind. It can be tempting to just call it quits and move on. Innovators are motivated to tackle the thorny challenges everyone else shies away from. To innovate, you need to believe there is always a way to get to the goal—even when everyone is telling you it's a lost cause. And then you need to convince others to believe.

The will to win is developed through practice, through competition, and through learning to overcome failure. Yet we live in an era where competition is being diluted in the name of making everyone feel good. Take the example of youth sports. Which is better for the development of young people: having kids play sports but not keeping score and everyone gets a medal? Or keeping score and only the winners get a trophy? What message are we sending to the participants in each scenario? What beliefs are we imparting? Which approach will better prepare them for the real world? I've coached youth sports in leagues where we didn't keep score and in competitive leagues where only the winners got trophies. I always found it interesting that even when we didn't keep score, the kids always knew who won. In my experience, it wasn't the kids who struggled with winning and losing—it was the parents. I believe kids are far more comfortable dealing with the facts than we give them credit for. I think the same is true for most adults.

While I understand the merit of building someone's confidence, the real world simply doesn't work that way. Are we really helping kids grow and overcome challenges when we don't have them deal with the brutal truths about the game they're playing? The objective of the game is to win, not just try hard. If you or your team loses, that's motivation to find a way to win the next time, or the next. Learning to find motivation in failure is critical to innovation.

I've heard the argument that we should want kids to play for the love of the game. I agree. But that doesn't require them to ignore the fact that it is a competition. In fact, I believe that competition and understanding that there is a winner and a loser are the foundation of learning to love the game. It's realizing that you have the ability to take your experience and use it to achieve a different outcome the next time. It's embracing the joy of taking on a challenge and working with a team to overcome obstacles and find a way to achieve the goal. You'll recall that I earlier shared the story of how we would ask people interviewing for jobs at Cree to play basketball with us. That became a way for us to identify who had the will to win—and to do whatever was needed to get there. We wanted to hire people who enjoyed the competition. If you love the game in this way, then the outcome really doesn't matter, but you will also never stop pursuing success. Dealing with reality head-on, instead of avoiding it or pretending it doesn't matter, is what the innovator's spirit is about.

THE WILL TO FLY

Can you imagine tackling a feat most people thought was impossible? How do you think you'd react if naysayers told you that you were just wasting your time, or even said that you were some kind of nutcase? Do you think you'd keep pushing through to the end, or would it be easier to just give up and go home?

Now try and imagine what it was like for Orville and Wilbur Wright, two brothers from Dayton, Ohio, who had become infected with the dream that they could take to the air like birds—at a time when national newspapers like the *Washington Post* were declaring: "It is a fact that man cannot fly."[1]

The Wrights were undaunted by the critics; they had a goal in mind—to build an aircraft that could take them into the sky. As the historian David McCullough writes in his book *The Wright Brothers*: "What the two had in common above all was unity of purpose and unyielding determination. They had set themselves on a mission."[2]

After becoming entrepreneurs at an early age—they had started a newspaper and a bicycle company—the Wrights became infatuated with the idea of flight. They read everything they could about the gliding pioneers who came before them, as well as about the biological engineering that birds used to take flight. Eventually, they made their way several hundred miles east to the windy sand dunes of Kitty Hawk on the Outer Banks of North Carolina to test their prototype of a glider. What they learned during several years of testing their designs was that much of what they had learned from the pioneers who came before them—such as the ideal length or curvature of wings—was wrong. They needed to discover what worked on their own.

Through experimentation and their own engineering skill, which included building their own wind tunnel, the brothers developed something they called "wing warping" that allowed them to keep their plane balanced in the air through subtle adjustments. Later, when they added a propeller powered by a four-cylinder engine, they also created a movable rudder to keep the plane steady. When the brothers thought they finally had a winning design, Wilbur won a coin toss to earn the honor of flying the plane first. Only, he yanked the rudder too hard on takeoff and crashed. Undeterred, the brothers repaired the plane and then, on December 17, 1903, Orville took off for twelve seconds in the first piloted flight of a power-driven, heavier-than-air plane—a flight that traveled 120 feet (each brother would perform two successful flights that day). As McCullough wrote:

> It had taken four years. They had endured violent storms, accidents, one disappointment after another, public indifference or ridicule, and clouds of demon mosquitoes. To get to and from their remote sand dune testing ground they made five round-trips from Dayton, a total of seven thousand miles by train, all to fly little more than half a mile. No matter. They had done it.[3]

The rest, as they say, is history, and our world has never been the same. But at first, not everyone was convinced the Wrights had achieved what they said they had. The naysayers continued to doubt them. It took Wilbur taking their plane to Europe in 1908, where he demonstrated the power of flight to thousands of awed onlookers—while giving rides to journalists and politicians—before the world truly understood the kind of innovation the Wrights had created. The one constant throughout that entire journey was their will to win.

WINNING AT WORK

While they weren't working toward a goal as lofty as manned flight, the innovators at Cree showed the same kind of spirit of determination to overcome the obstacles that popped up in their way. For example, in Cree's early days, the team was expanding the factory to support work on an important new research contract. This contract was critical to meet the company's revenue goals. To deliver on that contract, they needed to order and install special manufacturing equipment, but they found themselves running out of time to get it installed to meet the quarterly deadline. With just a few days to go until the contract deadline, the equipment arrived, but the city inspector wouldn't award a certificate of occupancy, or CO, until the specialty floor tiles were installed in the room where the equipment needed to go. That put everything on hold. The company was now at risk for missing its contract deadline, all because of some floor tiles. If the tile was not installed the next morning when the inspector came back, the equipment could not be installed and run, the contract could not be billed, and Cree would miss its goal.

Refusing to give up, people hit the phones, calling every tile supplier in the entire city. Nobody had what we needed. Eventually, after more calls and referrals, the team found someone who actually had the tiles in their warehouse. The catch was that the warehouse was in Virginia—about a six-hour drive away. The supplier also wouldn't deliver the tiles himself and he was about to close up for the day.

It's fair to say that most people would have begun to wave the white flag of surrender at this point. Not the innovators at Cree. People hit the phones again, this time calling taxi companies near the warehouse to see if they'd be willing to pick up the tile and drive it down to our factory that very night. Unbelievably, one taxi company agreed to make the delivery and, after driving through the night, arrived at the crack of dawn with the tile. The team then sprang into action to lay the tile before the inspector arrived. They pulled it off and got their CO, started up the equipment, and began work on the contract. The team met the goal.

If you want to innovate, you can't give up easily even in the face of what seems like insurmountable odds. Winning means not giving up; it means doing what it takes—and it can be infectious.

Imagine, for example, that you're working late in the office one night with a colleague and you realize that you left something you needed in a different room. But, when you go to retrieve the item, you realize that the door is locked—and you don't have the key. What do you do? You could call the facilities manager to open the door. But since it's late at night, you'd have to wait until the next day to get their help. What else could you do? I think it's fair to say that most people might just call it a day at this point and head home, right? Well, I found myself in this very scenario once when we were working on an important project. My colleague Scott and I were at work one weekend and I needed a folder from my office, but somehow it was locked with my keys inside. What did we do? We didn't give up and go home. I noticed that the office had a drop ceiling—the kind where there are tiles you can push up and out. So I had Scott stand on my shoulders—I'm six feet, six inches tall, for what it's worth—and then he popped up a tile on one side of the locked room and climbed up onto the top of the wall, removed a tile from the other side, and jumped down into the room and unlocked it from within. Problem solved! To me, that's the innovative spirit at work.

Of course, we all find ourselves confronting obstacles at work on a daily basis. What's your attitude when it comes to dealing with them? Are you willing to do what it takes to get on with your job, or would you rather call in someone to help instead? Consider the time that I walked into a meeting where everyone was sitting around a table staring at an empty screen. I was confused.

"What's going on?" I asked.

"The projector's not working," someone replied. "We called IT and we're waiting for someone to come and fix it."

"Did anyone try just turning it off and back on again?" I asked. No, they said, the projector was too hard to reach. Shaking my head, I climbed on top of the conference room table so I could reach the projector. I then flicked the switch on the back of the unit. Within seconds, the projector was back up and running and the meeting could begin. We all have more power than we think to overcome the obstacles that stand in our way. The innovator's spirit is about finding that willingness inside of you to find a solution—rather than just waiting around for someone else to solve the problem for you.

You can also think about what you might do if you face the same stakes that Compaq Computer cofounder Rod Canion faced in 1984.[4] At the time, Compaq had become one of the innovative leaders in what was then known as the "portable" personal computer market. But then IBM, the industry's five-hundred-pound gorilla, decided to get into the market as well. It looked like a death blow to the young company as orders from their distributors dried up overnight. Everyone was shifting to the new IBM computer instead. "We had this factory running full speed and nowhere to go," Canion told NPR interviewer Guy Raz. Facing a crisis, the team considered their options. They could scale back production, tighten their belts and cut temporary workers, and hope to ride things out. Or, more radically, they could continue to build inventory with the belief that the IBM computer wouldn't be as good as people thought it would be. According to Canion, they figured that if the IBM computer was better than theirs, they were dead anyway—so why not push ahead and keep building as a way to put themselves in a position to win in the long run? They had nothing to lose—and everything to win. So they built up their inventory of computers—even going so far as to rent several tractor trailers to store them in their parking lot. And you can probably guess what happened next. The IBM model didn't live up to expectations. It wasn't better than the Compaq. So new orders began to trickle back in and then increased to the point that they became a flood. "Everything fell into place and we took advantage of it," Canion said. By playing to win, Compaq reclaimed its leadership position in the industry (only to lose it again years later).

FINDING PLAYERS

We all know the saying "Everyone loves a winner." It's a notion that applies in sports and in business. When things are going great for a team or a company, everyone wants to be a part of it. We saw that at Cree after we became successful. When the business was making waves in the market and we were being lauded for our breakthrough products, everyone wanted to be on our team. The number of people applying for jobs went through the roof. But that also created a problem for us: How could we tell who had actually embraced their innovator's spirit and would stop at nothing, adjusting to the needs of the situation, to help reach our objectives? This was a real challenge.

To get past this, I would often ask job candidates: "Is your job title important to you?" It was an open-ended question that people generally reacted to in one of two ways. Some would respond that they didn't care what the title was, while others used the opportunity to reinforce the importance of their job title. It was one way for me to see if the person wanted to join our team for the right reasons. We never made an offer to someone who was worried about their job title. In our business, we were going to face tough challenges. I needed people who wanted to win and who couldn't care less about their title. They were the players that could get us to our goal.

As part of my screening process, I also would try to find an experience on a candidate's resume where the person had worked at a company that I had heard of. I'd research something that went wrong at the company and use that example to challenge the interviewee's will to win. In one example, I was interviewing a senior executive candidate who had worked at Kodak. After hearing about her many successes during her time there, I asked: "Didn't Kodak declare bankruptcy? Why didn't you do more to prevent that from happening?" She was shocked by my question. When she replied, she told me that she did what she could, but she wasn't responsible for those decisions. I challenged her further: "I realize you weren't making the final decision, but wasn't there something more you could have done to help the company succeed?" A spirited discussion ensued. I knew when we finished that day that she had the will to win. She wanted to compete and could be effective at Cree. What I learned years later was that she also remembered that conversation. Although she was initially put off by my questions, she was intrigued by the challenge and it made her more motivated to join the company.

The last thing I did in an interview was to try and get applicants to opt out by telling them they could work fewer hours and make more money elsewhere. I might have said something like: "I've enjoyed meeting with you today. As we wrap up, I want to give you some perspective. What we do here and how we go about it is not for everyone. We have unique values and very high expectations. We are trying to develop technology to solve problems that have never been solved before—technology that makes a difference. You will work harder here than at other companies, and they will pay you as much or more than we will. The reward is being part of something bigger than yourself. This company isn't for everyone, and I would ask that you seriously think about if it is the right place for you. If you end up joining our team, I promise that you will have the opportunity to challenge yourself and be part of something special—but you have to be willing to help make it happen." My goal in making these comments was to try to get the candidate to realize that it couldn't be about the money or the fame. They needed to want to compete. They needed to be playing for the love of the game.

To get hired at Cree, someone had to love the challenge and opportunity of trying to do something great. We didn't need people who wanted to say they were on the winning team or what their title was—those are fans. We needed people who wanted to do the work to help us win—we needed players who wanted to compete. What we were trying to do was hard; there were going to be numerous obstacles along the way. I wanted them to consider if they really valued the pursuit of innovation—did they have the will to win—and if they were willing to make the sacrifices to work in our company. If their heart wasn't in it, I wanted them to self-select out.

INVENTING THE FUTURE

When you fully embrace the competitive spirit that comes from a will to win, it can sometimes put you in situations you're not entirely comfortable with. No doubt you've heard the phrase "fake it until you make it." We hear about this kind of thing a lot in the technology world, where companies might market something they haven't actually built yet (which we call "vapor-ware"). While this kind of approach is risky, it can also be a source of incredible motivation to make something happen. I know because it happened early in my time at Cree.

I had been with the company for less than a year when my boss, Neal Hunter, walked into my office. At the time, we had the only commercially available blue LED in the world. He dropped a piece of paper on my desk. It was a faxed news release from a Japanese company that I had never heard of, announcing a new blue LED. At the time, our main product was a blue thirty-microwatt LED. The Japanese company was claiming they now had a blue LED that was fifty times brighter than ours—fifteen hundred microwatts—and it used completely different materials than we employed. It looked like we were in big trouble. This new product had the ability to kill our LED business just as it was getting started. It could also severely jeopardize the future of the company. I had just moved my family across the country to join this small company making blue LEDs, and all of a sudden, the future wasn't looking very bright.

Maybe he saw the look of concern on my face, because Neal then said, "Don't worry; we have a plan." Neal told me that he had just met with John, our chief LED scientist, and he and his team had already been experimenting with similar materials on a project to develop an ultraviolet laser diode. John was confident they could use what they'd learned on that project to develop a product to match the Japanese LED's brightness. Neal told me the team had committed to have the new LED completed in six months.

"OK," I said. "What can I do to help?"

"I want you to go out and start getting orders for our new LED," he told me.

Again, I must have looked confused. "How am I supposed to sell something that doesn't exist yet? Something that I don't even have the specs for?" I asked.

Neal smiled and said, "That's why I'm here. We're going to create those specs now."

We sat down at my Mac Classic computer and created a slide presentation and spec sheet for the new LED we were calling the DH85. Of course, everything I had written down was what we "hoped" we were going to invent. We believed it was possible. So, everything would come down to our team's ability to find a way to push through the obstacles in their way and create the new LED in the timeframe we were promising. A few days later, I bought an airplane ticket to Asia and headed out to start selling our new product that only existed on the slides we had just created and in the minds of our technical team. The customers were excited to hear about our new product and eager to get samples and place orders.

Our intent wasn't to mislead anyone. Rather, our goal was to put something out there and to embrace the belief that we would find a way to get to the goal—which we did. Six months after we received that fax, we started shipping samples of our new DH85 blue LED—and the race for who could make the next-brightest blue LED was on.

THE NEED FOR ETHICS

Doing what it takes to achieve the goal was a core value of Cree. We didn't spend much time talking about it; we just did it. As the company grew and we added many new employees, we realized the need to be more intentional about teaching the beliefs and behaviors that drove innovation. I was part of a leadership development program we created to help better define that connection. You can imagine my shock when "find a way to win" came up as a concern among the new hires. What I learned in these conversations was that this idea of doing whatever it took was sometimes being used to justify taking a shortcut, or to explain why something didn't work, or to do something that wasn't in the best interest of the company. It was being used as an excuse. It occurred to me during these discussions that what was missing was context and a commitment to continue to train both the leaders and the team members on our intent and hold them accountable. I had never imagined that doing what it takes and doing the right thing weren't fundamentally connected. One does not exist without the other. I had never considered someone would take this incredibly powerful belief and use it in the wrong way. I was able to explain in those sessions at Cree that all our beliefs and behaviors were connected—and by connecting them they work together and cannot be used by themselves as an excuse. I also would emphasize that if someone needs to be told that we expect everyone to act in an ethical, moral, and legal manner, they shouldn't be working for our company in the first place.

Consider what happens when this dynamic gets out of balance. The news contains plenty of examples of leaders betraying people's trust to further their own egos and agendas. Then, there are people who take the "fake it until you make it" approach and manipulate the spirit of it to justify not delivering on their promise. A prime example that comes to mind is the story of Elizabeth Holmes, the founder of the blood-testing company Theranos. Until a few years ago, Holmes was lauded around the world as a pioneering innovator who was transforming the way we could test for health and illnesses. Unlike the traditional blood-testing methods that required vials of blood to be drawn from a person's arm, Holmes had helped create a device that purportedly could run a wide range of some 240 tests—from cholesterol to cancer—on a single pinprick of blood. And the results were nearly instantaneous: just fifteen minutes, compared to hours or even days from more traditional testing methods. She named her invention the Edison. Holmes, whose name is on nineteen of the company's patents, received incredible fanfare for her device and the company she started. A story about a college dropout from Stanford who had started the next great tech company was almost too good to believe. She soon had raised millions of dollars from multiple big-name investors and politicians. It wasn't long before Holmes's face was on the cover of magazines like *Fortune* touting her rise as one of the world's few female billionaires. Holmes talked about how she idolized Steve Jobs, even going so far as to wear the similar black turtlenecks on a daily basis as Jobs did. It seemed like Holmes was on her way to becoming the world's next great innovator. That is, until everything fell apart. It was, in fact, all too good to be true.

An investigative reporter for *The Wall Street Journal* named John Carreyrou first broke the story that Holmes and Theranos weren't everything they were claiming to be.[5] (Carreyrou would later write a book called *Bad Blood: Secrets and Lies in a Silicon Valley Startup*, which then became the basis for an HBO documentary called *The Inventor*).[6] Perhaps most damning, it turned out that the Edison was actually giving people incorrect results—incorrectly telling people they had cancer, for example. But Theranos denied these reports— even as it began running its blood tests on traditional machines. Eventually, Theranos collapsed like a house of cards—costing investors millions. Holmes was charged with several crimes and, as I was writing this book, awaiting trial.

I share this story to point out that the will to win doesn't mean abandoning your ethics or moral compass. The ends do not justify the means when it comes to rationalizing bad behavior like lying or bad intentions. Did Holmes truly believe her company was on its way to making good on its promise? We may never know the full truth (she pleaded not guilty to the charges against her). But what we do know is that Holmes was not someone who reflected the true beliefs and behaviors of an innovator. While she might have initially been involved in the development of the Edison, she clearly seemed to distance herself from the work of perfecting the device and shifted more to promoting the company and herself. As I'll show you in the next chapter, I don't believe that Holmes appreciated the power that comes from getting your hands dirty as an innovator. While innovations require good marketing to get the world interested, marketing alone cannot turn an idea into an innovation.

CHAPTER FOUR RECAP

Belief: There is always a way to get to the goal.

Behavior: Find a way to win.

KEY INSIGHTS

Find the will to win. Innovation is about constantly overcoming challenges. You have to believe there is always a way and be willing to do what it takes to succeed.

Play for the love of the game. You need players, not fans. You need people who want to compete and are looking for the opportunity to try and do something great.

Invent the future. Somebody has to be first and willing to put an idea out there and then embrace the belief that they will find a way to get to the goal.

CHAPTER FIVE

Get Your Hands Dirty

"If a cluttered desk is a sign of a cluttered mind,
of what, then, is an empty desk a sign?"
—Albert Einstein[1]

HAVE YOU EVER NOTICED THE companies that promote innovation in their advertising? Can you think of a recent example? Nissan, for instance, seems to have made innovation part of its TV and print ads over the past several years. I recall one tagline saying, "Innovation That Excites" and, more recently, an ad that says, "Innovation for All." I like good advertising as much as anyone else. But I'm always skeptical of companies that spend their time telling you how innovative they are. In my experience, the more a company uses the words *innovation, innovate,* or even *invent* in its public statements and media, the more likely it is that the company is not innovative at all. Why? If someone can't recognize that something is innovative without you telling them, it's probably not innovative.

Let's get back to my Nissan example. This is the same company that designed the Nissan Juke. If you have ever seen this car, you would remember it—but not for the right reasons. I have no idea what they were thinking, but I don't see any innovation. Is it an odd-looking little car? Absolutely. Is it innovative? Absolutely not. I recently bought a new Nissan Murano. It is a nice car, but I have yet to find anything innovative about it.

As someone who worked at Hewlett-Packard, I became just as disillusioned by the "HP Invent" marketing campaign. To be fair, they said "Invent," not "Innovate." But once again, I didn't see anything new—let alone innovative. When Bill Hewlett and Dave Packard were building the company, you could see the innovation with your own eyes. Nobody had to tell you.

What I've learned time and again is that successful innovators don't spend their time talking about how innovative they are, because they're focused on actually doing it. Innovation doesn't come from marketing—it comes from getting your hands dirty and solving problems that create real value. You can't delegate innovation.

One of the reasons people struggle to lead innovation is because, at its core, innovation is messy. It's inefficient at times and if you want to uncover answers, you need to be personally willing to get your hands dirty. All too often, managers and, frankly, many executives think they can sit in their office and order people to just go "innovate." Have you ever sat down with your team and done their job or helped them do their job? Why or why not? What was the benefit to the team? What was the benefit to you?

When we were struggling with a problem in our business, I would go to the problem. To do that, I would spend time with the team in the factory or in the labs, listening, observing, and asking questions. I wasn't the expert, but I was ultimately responsible for our success (or failure). I knew that the answers usually were hidden in the details. Was I going to find the answer? Unlikely. But getting into the details with our team changed the dynamic. As the person who knew enough to ask questions but not enough to know the answers, I could ask the questions that usually led to other questions that eventually led the team to make a connection that wasn't there before. As some of my team would say, I knew just enough to be dangerous.

If you want to tap into your innovator's spirit and lead innovation, you have to get up close and personal with it. You need to understand the situation enough that you can help connect dots that others might not otherwise be able to see.

HANDS-ON INNOVATION

If I asked you to picture a motorcycle, what kind of image would immediately come to mind? I think for most of us, our brains would draw up a big, burly-looking machine with the words "Harley-Davidson" scrawled on its side. While there are plenty of different kinds and brands of motorcycles out there, there is just something iconic about the Harley-Davidson look and brand—what bike enthusiasts call a "chopper" or even a "hog." The roar of a Harley gunning down the highway, its rider smiling as they rev the throttle, is hard to forget.

What you might not know is that when the company got its start in 1901, the innovators behind the brand—twenty-one-year-old William Harley and twenty-two-year-old Arthur Davidson—had a lot to figure out on their own.[2] At the time, before the surge in popularity of the automobile a few decades later, the bicycle had become a ubiquitous feature on the streets of cities like Milwaukee, Wisconsin, where the young entrepreneurs lived. It was also in Milwaukee where, in 1895, an Englishman named Edward Pennington demonstrated the world's first bicycle powered by an engine: a motorcycle.[3]

It was not long after that Harley and Davidson set out to create a motorcycle of their own. When Arthur's brother, Walter—who was already an accomplished bicycle racer—joined the fledgling company, they created two working prototypes. They began to enter early motorcycle races to show how their bike was better than the competition. In particular, they wanted to prove that their design was built tough—and that it was capable of taking someone anywhere they wanted to go. American roads of that era were rarely paved and full of potholes. Building a bike that withstood punishment, especially at high speeds, was critical to making the motorcycle a practical transportation solution. What made Harley and Davidson innovative was that they were solving a key problem for their customers: "[It was] less trouble and expense than a horse, and requiring less exertion than a bicycle."[4] In other words, they were providing customers with a reliable source of transportation.

With more than one hundred different motorcycle competitors at the time, the Harley-Davidson team used the races as a way to stand out. Walter's victory in a race held in Chicago in 1905 helped earn the company plenty of publicity, which, in turn, helped them land their first dealership partner—where the first three production bikes they ever made were sold in 1906.[5]

But as with any early invention, the bike and its engine ran into difficulties—including an occasional oil leak or fire—which Harley and the three Davidsons (another brother, Bill, also joined the company) tackled by fixing with their own hands, and later with their production teams to make modifications. It was said that Bill "would always remain in close touch with the workers on the floor, no matter how big the company got, using their insights to make constant improvements."[6]

Even when everything looks good on paper and when something should work, sometimes it just doesn't when you're innovating. That's why the Harley-Davidson team listened to the requests of their potential customers and constantly tweaked and revised the bike's original design to make it better and more powerful over time. And because they rode their bikes themselves—with Walter continuing to compete in races as long as one thousand miles— they learned which features actually benefited the customer and which ones they could eliminate. They were literally getting their hands dirty and their elbows greasy as they turned an invention into the kind of innovation you now see on a daily basis. The company became known as the industry's leading innovator by introducing the first clutch, the three-speed transmission, the carburetor choke, and the step-starter.[7] Interestingly, within just a few decades, all of the company's competitors had gone out of business while the Harley-Davidson brand would become renowned worldwide. But getting from there to here wasn't exactly a straight line because . . .

INNOVATION IS MESSY

And that doesn't just apply to making motorcycles. Sometimes getting your hands dirty can quite literally lead to breakthroughs.

Studies show that the messier an environment is, the more innovative people become. For example, one study split a group of forty-eight American students into two rooms: one neat and ordered and the other messy and cluttered. The students were asked to come up with new innovative uses for regular ping-pong balls. The researchers then recruited a panel of judges to weigh in on which ideas were the most creative. In the end, the students who worked in the messy room came up with the better ideas. While the "clean team" came up with ideas like using the balls to play beer pong, the "messy" team suggested ideas like using the balls as ice-cube trays or attaching them to the bottoms of furniture legs to protect floors.[8] "While cleaning up certainly has its benefits, clean spaces might be too conventional to let inspiration flow," said Kathleen Vohs, a psychological scientist and marketing professor at the University of Minnesota who conducted the study. Vohs also noted that a separate study conducted at Northwestern University found that people placed in a messy room drew more creative pictures and were quicker to solve a challenging brainteaser puzzle than people working in a tidy room.

But we only have to look back at some of the more life-changing events in history for proof that innovation is truly messy. Consider that penicillin, one of the world's early antibiotics, was "discovered" by Alexander Fleming because he accidentally allowed some mold to grow in a petri dish he was using.[9] He had forgotten to put the dish, which he was growing bacteria in, into a sanitary vault before he left on vacation. Classic move for a spacey scientist, right? When he returned, he noticed the mold. But rather than toss it away, he decided to get his hands dirty and take a closer look under a microscope. He noticed that the mold had actually killed the bacteria. As he would later write: "When I woke up just after dawn on September 28, 1928, I certainly didn't plan to revolutionize all medicine by discovering the world's first antibiotic, or bacteria killer. But I guess that was exactly what I did."[10]

Or consider how Charles Goodyear discovered how to make vulcanized rubber—the stuff our cars' tires are made of.[11] The problem at the time was that anything made of organic rubber—which is really just tree sap—would eventually melt into a gelatinous glob. Goodyear, who had become fascinated by the substance at the ripe age of thirty-four, decided to become a self-taught chemist. He began a years-long experimentation on how to improve rubber—including during a stint when he was jailed for his debts.[12] But despite numerous setbacks with his various odorous experiments—such as trying to cook the rubber with nitric acid or by mixing it with magnesia and quicklime—nothing worked. The rubber would still eventually melt.

After years of struggling and living in near destitution while he provided for his family by catching fish out of New York Harbor, Goodyear finally experienced some good fortune. He had begun experimenting with adding sulfur to his rubber when he accidently dripped some on a hot stove. When he bent down to examine the result, he soon realized he had created a waterproof and durable rubber. While history has dubbed this a true "accident," Goodyear credited his ability to make a new connection others hadn't seen, or as he put it, "[his mind was] prepared to draw an inference." He was ready to make the discovery because he had been getting his hands dirty for a long time. It also highlights the value in having knowledge about many different areas, which helps enable the ability to make these connections.

Even then it took him another year of experimentation—and another stint in debtor's prison—to perfect what would become known as the vulcanized rubber process. Interestingly, the public was first introduced to Goodyear's rubber in men's shirts, where it was woven with cloth to create the ruffled shirtfronts that were all the rage at that time. Innovations don't always begin where you think they will.

If you were walking through our offices at Cree, how would you have identified the best innovators? What would you expect to see in their workspace? It's been my experience that the best innovators I worked with always had the messiest desks. One of our great innovators, a guy named Gerry, had a beard that made you think he played in the band ZZ Top when he wasn't at work. His office was a disaster. In fact, someone on our environment, health, and safety team actually tried to give him a safety violation for his office space. He had an extra chair in his office that he used to house stacks of paper that didn't fit on his desk or shelves. In addition to the various papers and books on his desk, you might find different chemicals or components he was conducting experiments with. But what looked like uncontrolled chaos was actually Gerry's way of finding connections between ideas no one had yet figured out. He was immersed in the details, getting his hands dirty coming up with new ideas to solve important problems—but it was messy.

I was someone who liked to clean my desk before I left each night. The ability to create a small sense of order at the end of the day was how I tried to deal with the chaos of running a large company and clear the canvas to be ready for the next day. But when I was in creative mode, the scene was quite different. Whether I was working through a change to our business strategy or trying to find a solution to the challenge of the week, my desk quickly gathered stacks of information from all different sources as I sorted through the details to try to put the pieces together in a way that solved the problem.

NEAT AND TIDY DOESN'T WORK

But not everyone has learned this lesson. Just think about what's happened to the pharmaceutical industry in recent years. It faces enormous pressure to constantly bring new products to market to help replace existing drugs whose patents expire. And to do that, pharmaceutical companies must follow very strict and rigid rules set by the government—which creates pressure to try to make innovation a process that is anything but messy. And likely also why their return on R&D investment continues to tumble.

I remember interviewing a bright lawyer for our general counsel position who had been the lead counsel for the R&D group at a major pharmaceutical company. I asked him how his old firm drove innovation, and he told me that he was part of a cross-functional team of researchers, lawyers, and marketing and finance experts—what they called an "innovation council"—that vetted any new ideas the R&D team came up with. He was proud of the billions of dollars his employer had spent in its drug development efforts. The council's role, he explained, was to vet the ideas to see which ones were most likely to result in a new product. They were optimized for likelihood of success, not potential benefit. Any idea that seemed too far-fetched or high risk was eliminated, and those that remained were given the OK to try and bring to market. I could tell that he really thought this approach was a great idea. He was a lawyer, so I understand why he wanted to reduce risk. That's what he was trained to do. I thought to myself, *This is a horrible idea. If you reduce the risk to increase the chance of success, you also reduce the potential for innovation—they're wasting the time and money.* So I asked him what breakthrough products they had come up with during his time. I knew the answer, but I couldn't help myself. He hesitated a moment before answering. "We didn't come up with any breakthroughs," he admitted. This is exactly my point: Innovation is messy, so why were people uncomfortable with it involved in this process in the first place?

As the largest pharmaceutical companies have tried to make drug development safer and more predictable, they've also made it more expensive and less effective. A 2018 study by the consulting firm Deloitte found that the cost to develop new drugs continues to soar: The average cost of bringing a new product to market costs more than $2 billion, up from $800 million in 2010, even though the average drug is expected to earn just $400 million in new revenue.[13] So these pharma companies are getting fewer returns from spending all that money. That same year, the world's twelve largest drug companies earned a return of a mere 1.9 percent—down from 10.1 percent nine years earlier.[14]

The pace of new drugs hitting the market has also plummeted. Another study cited in *Fortune* magazine found that the thirty large and small pharmaceutical and biotech companies it researched earned just eleven percent of their revenue from drugs that they had developed in the past five years. Talk about a crisis in innovation.[15] As an industry analyst frames the issue: "Ignoring the stochastic nature of drug development has led to costly mistakes and, ultimately, the industry's decline."[16] At these levels of return on R&D, it seems clear these companies are incapable of effective innovation. I don't know of many industries that are able to be this ineffective and not be forced to change their approach. But change is coming. It may take longer than some would like, but innovation will eventually find this inefficiency and force the industry to change.

You can't really control innovation or turn it into a predictable and manageable process. You have to allow for some accidental discoveries along the way. As Bill Coyne, who led the innovation efforts at the company 3M for many years, once said:

> [Don't] try to control or make safe the fumbling, panicky, glorious adventure of discovery. Occasionally, one sees articles that describe how to rationalize this process, how to take the fuzzy front end and give it a nice haircut. This is self-defeating. We should allow the fuzzy front end to be as unkempt and as fuzzy as we can. Long-term growth depends on innovation, and innovation isn't neat. We stumble on many of our best discoveries. If you want to follow the rapidly moving leading edge, you must learn to live on your feet. And you must be willing to make necessary, healthy stumbles.[17]

THE DETAILS MATTER

Would you ever consider the rock band Van Halen to be innovators? They certainly left their mark on the world of music with songs featuring Eddie Van Halen's guitar and the on-stage antics of their original lead singer, David Lee Roth—"Diamond Dave." But it turns out that Van Halen practiced an essential trait every innovator needs: an attention to detail.

One thing rock stars like Roth have been known for through the ages is their eccentricities—especially when it comes to odd additions to their contracts. Many people scoffed, for instance, when they heard that one of the clauses in Van Halen's contracts was that there needed to be a bowl of M&M's backstage at every concert. Worse, the rider in the contract stated: "WARNING: ABSOLUTELY

NO BROWN ONES."[18] The band could literally walk away from a concert if they found a brown M&M backstage. Crazy rock stars, right? Not quite. It turns out that there was a reason for that clause. The band wanted to make sure people actually read the details of the contract. If the band noticed a brown M&M in the bowl, they figured other details might have been overlooked, not just in the contract, but in how the venue handled the entire production of the show.

I also tried hard to keep an eye on the details with our innovation efforts. One way I did that was by bringing our LED lights back home and testing them with my family to determine if they were really as good as we claimed. I was drinking the "Kool-Aid" each day and I needed to see for myself if our products were as good as we thought. Before we even got into the lighting business, I had ordered ten LED downlights from one of our new customers (LLF). LLF was started by Neal Hunter (after leaving Cree) and a couple of former Cree scientists. They had created an innovative LED downlight—a six-inch can light that is installed in a ceiling—that could replace the traditional incandescent or compact fluorescent (CFL) lighting products (those squiggly looking bulbs). I had the lights installed in my kitchen right before we hosted a party for our friends. I remember being very excited about all the attention these new lights were going to get—especially since light in a kitchen can be so revealing. The wood grain of a cabinet door, the veins on a granite countertop, and even the color of a piece of fruit can change drastically based on the quality of the light shining on it. This was going to be great: I could finally show my friends that LED lighting was real and coming to a home near them. And yet, as the party continued, I kept waiting for someone to say something about our new lights, but no one did. They didn't notice a difference. Everyone left that evening and I was pretty disappointed. On Monday morning, I called Neal to tell him what happened. After a pause, he told me: "That was the best compliment you could have given me. The fact that nobody noticed that the lights were different meant that they were just as good as the incandescent bulbs. That means the product really works." Wow, I thought. He's right. No one noticed—which was pretty effective at building my confidence that we were truly on to something innovative. And I wouldn't have really understood what was coming without seeing the results—the details—with my own eyes.

INSIGHT TO ASK QUESTIONS

Not only is innovation messy—it's very personal, which provides a different context to getting your hands dirty. In my time at Cree, that fact that I kept myself involved in the details at all levels of the organization gave me insights that were critical to fueling my innovator's spirit. If you're not close enough to see and hear the problems, you're not going to be able to help resolve them or find the connections that allow you to move beyond them.

That's why I sat in on R&D reviews at Cree even when I was CEO. I wasn't there to micromanage anyone. I wanted to listen and learn where the technology was headed. I didn't want to just get a report from someone about what we were doing; I needed to understand what was happening with my own eyes and ears. If you operate only at thirty thousand feet, you'll miss details that could help you eliminate barriers that might be slowing up the process and you'll miss opportunities to help the team adjust course when new information emerges that changes the rules.

An example of the benefits of this approach occurred during the development of the Cree LED bulb. A small team was working in secret at an off-site location to develop the bulb. The team operated outside the normal management structure of the company, with the leader reporting directly to me on the project's progress every one or two weeks. I would usually have a chance to see the latest samples and test them for myself. During one of these meetings, Neal (who was leading the team) mentioned that they had hit a roadblock. To make the Cree LED bulb achieve the lifetime goals we had set, we had to reduce the heat generated in the bulb. To do this, we were going to need to double the number of LED chips in the design, thereby doubling the cost of the LEDs. If we added all of the LEDs, the bulb would cost more than the price we were going to sell it for. The math didn't work. This was a big problem, but after thinking about it for a few minutes, I had a solution. I had previously spent a lot of time understanding the details of how our factory worked and developing our cost model with the finance team. As a result, I knew that most of our factory costs were fixed. In other words, those costs were the same whether we made more products or fewer products. I also knew that we had excess capacity. Making more LEDs would only cost a small fraction of the normal cost, and much less than what the finance team's cost model said they would be. They were basically free. So, I told the team to assume the extra LEDs were free and to keep going with the project. The extra LEDs we would need for the project weren't exactly free, but close enough for what we were trying to do. It was my personal knowledge of how the factory costs worked that gave me this insight.

On a related note, our original concept for the LED bulb entailed filling it with gas to transfer the heat generated by the LEDs to the glass and away from the bulb. It was a great concept and looked just like a regular light bulb. But after further testing, we realized it didn't work as expected—and the team was stuck. We had already gotten approval from the board for this project and had a purchase commitment from the largest retailer of light bulbs. In my conversation with Neal that week, I asked why we couldn't just add a heat sink—a piece of metal or other thermally conductive material—in the bulb to draw the heat away like many other LED bulbs out there. I remembered our team had used this concept in a prototype bulb we had demonstrated a couple of years earlier. Doing that would keep the look and feel of a regular light bulb and get rid of the heat. Neal took the suggestion and went back to work with the team, and in the end, it worked. If I hadn't been involved in the details of how things worked, I could have never made the suggestion. Neal and his team would have likely figured it out on their own, but by getting my hands dirty, I was able to help them find the solution a little faster.

PROVIDE PERSPECTIVE

In addition to insight, the details provide important perspective. Being in the details with the team gave me context and allowed me to provide context to others. In 2009, our quest to make LED lighting a reality got a little more personal. I was invited to the White House with several other CEOs as part of President Barack Obama's efforts to push the spread of green, energy-saving technology around the country. The meeting almost didn't happen, since the first time the White House called and talked with my assistant, she thought it was a prank. Why would the White House possibly be calling me? She took a number and said she would call back. When she did, the White House switchboard answered, and we realized that this was for real. At the time, the country was in a terrible economic recession, and the president was looking to "green technology" as something that was both good for the economy and good for the environment. Legislation had been passed that created new standards to increase lighting efficiency, which was exactly what LED lighting was designed to do. I have to admit, I was a bit nervous being invited to the White House to meet with the president. When we arrived, we were shown into the Roosevelt Room for our meeting. I looked around and noticed that there weren't any LED lights installed there. The president hadn't arrived quite yet, so I asked Steven Chu, the Secretary of Energy at the time, why they weren't using LED lighting. And he told me something I have never forgotten. He said: "LEDs won't be relevant until they pay for themselves in my lifetime—not the LEDs' lifetime." His comment left a mark on me that day. I wrote it down and hung it on a wall in my office, right above my desk. He was right! It was personal now and his words became a constant source of motivation as we continued to push the technology forward—he reminded me that creating value was the ultimate test of innovation—and we weren't there yet. It has been about a decade since that meeting and I'm happy to report that LED lights now pay for themselves in about a year. I hope that Secretary Chu has noticed.

While getting your hands dirty is critical to discovering your innovator's spirit, we need to take a step back and look at how you get started. How do you create the future?

CHAPTER FIVE RECAP

Belief: The answers often lie in the details.

Behavior: Get your hands dirty.

KEY INSIGHTS

Innovation is messy. Innovation doesn't fit into neat and tidy processes. If you want to uncover answers, you need to be personally willing to get your hands dirty.

The details matter. The answers to problems are usually hidden in the details. They provide the insights that enable you to connect the dots.

Perspective is critical. It is easy to lose sight of the big picture. Stay focused on what really matters to achieve the goal.

CHAPTER SIX

You Create the Future

"The best way to predict the future is to create it."
—Abraham Lincoln[1]

HAS SOMEONE EVER CHALLENGED YOU to "think outside the box"? I'll bet they have. But what exactly does that mean? Let's first start with the definition. It is a metaphor that means to think differently, unconventionally, or from a new perspective. This seems like a good starting point if you want to pursue innovation. And there is a lot written on the topic, some of which I've read—but most of which I've ignored. Based on my experience, there are plenty of consultants selling advice on how you can "think outside the box." Let me save you some time and money. It's the wrong starting point. Why? Let's start with the box itself. What is the box? Is it real or is it imagined? Are you dealing with a box that someone else has created or a box of your own making? Keep in mind, we're trying to uncover your innovator's spirit. Still thinking about the box?

Let me give you a hint: There is no box.

Whatever box you're "in" only exists because you've allowed it to exist. It's a choice you've made, which means you can choose differently. So what is this box that's getting in our way? In its simplest form, the box is a set of boundary conditions that affect your approach to a problem or new idea. These could be deeply held beliefs or rules that you've come to accept as not changeable. I was discussing this concept with my son, Chuck, who's a college student, and he summarized the problem this way: "Thinking about a box in any way, shape, or form leaves you vulnerable to being trapped in the box or the past." He's right. The box is a trap that limits what is possible. If you want to innovate, you need to believe that there is no box.

The challenge is that we live in a world full of boxes. We've been taught rules and expectations of what is or is not possible, and learned that there are negative repercussions for trying something outside the box. The box is all around us, and it starts at an early age. One of the first things we teach young children is to color within the lines. Why? Because in our mind those are the rules. When left to their own creativity, most kids just color all over the page. We're forcing them inside a box.

I was making this point a couple of years ago and someone asked me, "So what do you do when you're stuck in the box?" I replied, "Set the box on fire." Maybe it's not the best analogy, but if the box is on fire, people will have to make a choice. Get burned by the fire or get out. Our basic human survival instinct is incredibly strong. The fight-or-flight response kicks in and you'll find a way out of the box. Also, by setting the box on fire, it will be burned down. It goes away. No more box. You're free to imagine a different future— one you can create. This journey to uncover your innovator's spirit is about getting rid of your boxes—the conditions you place on yourself that get in the way of doing something new.

Let me give you a personal example of how your thinking can change when you set your box on fire. I had been the CEO of Cree for about four or five years when my oldest daughter, Kim, started looking at colleges. It is one of those life moments that you're not really prepared for. At some point it dawned on me: She's leaving home in a short time. I had been working so much over the past eighteen years that I hadn't had time to process it. I had been too busy trying to build the company, living in my CEO box. And I realized that it was a problem. I had missed so much of her life growing up because I often put work ahead of family events like ballet recitals. We took vacations, but only when I could squeeze them into my schedule. That's what CEOs do, right? That's how you make the company successful. That was my box talking. So I made a decision. I was still going to do everything possible to make Cree successful, but I needed to figure out a way to also enjoy time with my kids while I still could. We had another year before college, and there were still two kids at home. I had two more opportunities to create a different reality. This was my chance. I decided that vacations would become a priority, time for me to be completely in the moment with my family. I was going to find a way to be a fully committed CEO and a more engaged parent. What did that look like? I went to work a little earlier each morning, and many afternoons, I would leave for a couple of hours to coach baseball or basketball practice. Then I would head back to work, or return home and work later into the evening. I learned to be more focused at work, trust the team more, and get a little less sleep. And I think I became a better leader. Taking a break gave me time to think, got me out of my CEO box, and helped me see new possibilities. It also helped me realize that there is no box, unless you allow one to exist. It is a choice.

BEYOND THE BOX

You're probably thinking to yourself, so there is no box. Great. Now what? How do I apply this idea to innovation? The challenge innovators face is finding ways to help people see the possibility of something beyond the boundaries of their current box-limited reality. This sounds cool (and it is when it works), but it can be really hard. What we learned at Cree over the years is that inventing something is often the easy part; making it relevant to others can be a much bigger challenge.

Consider the rise of the craft beer movement in the United States. At last count, the number of craft brewers around the country has climbed to more than seven thousand. Chances are, wherever you live, there's a brewery. But that wasn't always the case. While the United States has a long history of homebrewing dating back to Benjamin Franklin and George Washington, who brewed beer using their own recipes, it all disappeared during Prohibition—which lasted from 1920 until its repeal in 1933. Only the larger brewers who were capable of shifting their business to new markets like milk and yogurt survived. For context: There were some four thousand breweries in the United States in 1873. By the 1970s, a century later, fewer than one hundred breweries were left. And they all made similar beer—mostly tame lagers and pilsners. If you wanted anything else, you needed to find an import from Europe. A few enterprising entrepreneurs in California like Fritz Maytag at Anchor Brewing (which still exists today) and Jack McAuliffe at New Albion Brewing Company (which went out of business) tried to make different beer. But they couldn't seem to convince the majority of consumers it was really better than what the big brewers were making. As Maytag, an heir to the appliance fortune of that name, once said: "If you want to make a small fortune brewing beer, start with a large fortune."[2]

Then something changed. Strangely enough, it was a law signed in 1978 by President Jimmy Carter—a lifelong teetotaler—that made homebrewing legal again. This law inspired a new generation of fans to take up homebrewing, including Fred Eckhardt and Charlie Papazian, who wrote hugely influential books like *A Treatise on Lager Beers* and *The Complete Joy of Homebrewing*, respectively, that fueled others to brew their own beer. (I purchased Papazian's book when I started on my own homebrewing adventure in 1989.)

But the idea that craft beer could ever go mainstream seemed impossible. Well, except to another homebrewer named Jim Koch, a former management consultant who decided to turn his great-great-grandfather's beer recipe into a new business in 1984: The Boston Beer Company.

The seeds of inspiration for starting his business were planted years before when Koch was an undergrad at Harvard University. It was during a class discussion of scientist Thomas Kuhn's paradigm shifts that Koch says he was hit by a revelation: "We only think we know what we know, and that most of our assumptions at any point in time are wrong and will be revised."[3]

What Koch eventually realized in his time working as a management consultant was that most businesses operate in accepted paradigms where they merely make incremental improvements in cost or quality. Any attempt to challenge that paradigm is "always frowned upon or marginalized, dismissed as impractical or wrongheaded."[4] In other words, people don't like it when someone tells you there isn't a box.

But Koch recognized that and saw beyond it. He saw a different future for beer. He knew the accepted paradigm at that time in the 1980s was that small breweries could never compete with the big brewers. Koch came from a family of six generations of brewers, but his own father thought starting a brewery was a bad idea. He told his son: "Brewing today is about size—nothing else. You're crazy!"[5] (To be fair, Koch's father eventually became one of his first investors.)

Koch decided there was an opportunity to challenge that paradigm. As he writes in his 2016 book *Quench Your Own Thirst*: "The truth is that most of the value in an industry is created precisely by people who venture outside of conventional wisdom. You know the people I'm talking about—the ones who embrace the wondrously creative 'holy shit' moments and who go on to do what most people didn't expect or even think was possible."[6]

Koch's "holy shit" moment was that he saw a huge opportunity to build a brewery of his own:

> A new business is built on a different and better approach than what's already out there. And it's okay to enter a field you know only a little about, because that little bit you know can be key. Ignorance can actually be a huge asset, giving you the best vantage point. When I started

The Boston Beer Company, I had no serious beer industry experience on my side—only ignorance and Thomas
Kuhn. But that was a lot.[7]

In the beginning, Koch peddled his signature beer—Samuel
Adams lager—from bar to bar in Boston, encouraging barkeepers
to put his beer on tap next to those of the big brewers. Humble
beginnings to be sure. But eventually, Koch's work in convincing
consumers that his beer solved a real problem—namely that it
made beer taste good again—eventually helped spark the craft beer
revolution we enjoy to this day.

Another example of someone who ignored the box is Elon Musk
and Tesla Motors. While the big carmakers like General Motors
had been experimenting with electric vehicles for years (a history
that dates back to the 1800s), they failed to inspire any real interest
in them. They were trying to solve a real problem—a reliance on
fossil fuel to power a car—but they were going about it the wrong
way. The boxy and clunky vehicles they made like General Motors'
EV1 never took off. Even the hybrid Toyota Prius appealed to only
the so-called eco-warrior crowd. They knew the technology had
potential, but they were coming at the problem with the boundary
conditions of an internal combustion engine driven industry.

In the late 1990s, some of the bright engineering minds in
Silicon Valley began to uncover the potential of lithium ion bat-
teries, which could propel a car from zero to sixty miles an hour
in just 4.9 seconds. When the engineer turned serial entrepreneur
and investor Elon Musk, who had already earned a fortune as the
cofounder of PayPal, saw an early prototype of such a car made by
a company called AC Propulsion, he fell in love. The author of a
biography of Musk writes: "He saw its potential as a screaming-fast

machine that could shift the perception of electric cars from boring and plodding to something aspirational."[8] In other words, he understood the real problem worth solving: creating a high-performance car that looked great and that also allowed you to skip the gas station.

At that same time, two other engineers turned entrepreneurs, Martin Eberhard and Marc Tarpenning, who had invented and sold the technology behind one of the first e-readers, had also fallen for the idea of creating an electric car. They decided to form a new company in 2003, which they dubbed Tesla Motors, "both to pay homage to the inventor and electric motor pioneer Nikola Tesla and because it sounded cool."[9] They were then joined by an engineer named J. B. Straubel, who was a leading authority on lithium ion battery technology.

But the Tesla team was quickly reminded that the last successful start-up in the auto industry was Chrysler in 1925. Because of that, they didn't find a lot of interest among investors to back their effort—until they ran into Musk, who had already seen the real potential of all-electric cars. He quickly signed on by investing $6.5 million, which made him the largest shareholder and chair of the new business.

Even then, the odds against Tesla ever making a dent seemed enormous. As one biographer of Musk puts it: "Had anyone from Detroit stopped by Tesla Motors at this point, they would have ended in hysterics. The sum total of the company's automotive experience was that a couple of the guys at Tesla really liked cars and another one created a series of science fair projects based on technology that the automobile industry considered ridiculous."[10]

But the Tesla team wasn't about to be trapped by that box. They weren't even going to run their company like the other automakers.

Musk's biographer writes: "No, Tesla would do what every other Silicon Valley start-up had done before it, which was hire a bunch of young, hungry engineers and figure things out as they go along."[11]

You might argue that the road Tesla and Musk have traveled since then has been anything but straight and narrow. While the company has been plagued with numerous production issues over the years and Musk's quirky personality has put him in hot water from time to time, the company has changed the auto business forever. If you've ever driven or ridden in a Tesla, you know what I mean: It's like driving something from the future—which has forced the other automakers to try and play catch-up. The cars on our roads will never be the same again.

As yet another example of going beyond the box, think about the case of Linus Torvalds, a Finnish software programmer who, in 1991, became frustrated by the limitations of traditional computer operating systems. Not content with the status quo, he wanted to find a better way—a way out of the box when it came to the limitations of existing standards. So he posted a note on a global message board read by his fellow programmers that began with the words: "Hello everybody . . . I'm doing a (free) operating system (just a hobby, nothing big and professional . . .)."[12]

Whether he intended to or not, Torvalds's "hobby" sparked a revolution in the world of computer software that caused millions of interested programmers—most of whom volunteered their time—to join his open-source effort to create what we now know as the Linux operating system. In its different permutations, Linux is now among the most widely used software on the planet, powering everything from smartphones and TVs to cars and airplanes. At the same time, Torvalds created an entirely new way to go about creating software: Crowdsourcing had been born. It's been reported that it has taken some forty-one thousand person-years to create Linux—the equivalent of about $4 billion in developer salaries—all done by volunteers who didn't believe there was a box.[13] Now that's innovation in action.

SETTING THE BOX ON FIRE

When I talked with people who wanted to work at Cree, I would often ask, "If you were going to start a company to compete against your current company, what would you do?" After they thought about the question and provided some ideas, I would ask them: "So why haven't you done it already?" I almost always heard something like "I can't" or "They won't let me." They were describing their box.

I used the same question internally with our leadership team. My goal in asking questions like this was to break free of any box that might be trapping us based on the things we had done in the past that made us successful. It simply wasn't good enough to count on the fact that we could just keep doing those same things and remain successful. We had to be willing to constantly take a fresh look at the business. And when you can do that, and have the courage to do something about it, you can continue to drive innovation forward. But that's not always easy to do.

I remember a key moment in Cree's history where we faced this same challenge. At the time, we had built up a successful business selling LED chips that were then converted into white LEDs that were sold to big electronic companies who wanted them for backlighting monitors and TVs. We were then approached by one of the biggest players in the business, LG Electronics (LG). They wanted to form a joint venture to manufacture white LEDs to put inside their products. We had the technology, know-how, and intellectual property. They had the money to fund this new venture and demand for LEDs. This was a *huge* opportunity for us. Not only was LG offering to fund the new business, they were also willing to guarantee us a certain amount of profits for the next three years. It seemed like a lay-up—just tell us where to sign the contract, right?

While there was plenty of excitement about the deal, we also wanted to take an outside-in look at what this really meant for our future. What was going to happen in the next five to ten years? We saw what was happening in the industry and that the other big players were also moving in a similar direction as LG. They wanted to start a joint venture to build expertise, with the intent to eventually make their own LEDs. It would become a race to the bottom to see who could become the low-cost producer. The customers we had today would also become our competitors—which would make life even more difficult for us.

As we talked more about what we thought the future would look like, we saw that LED lighting would eventually emerge as the biggest market for LEDs—a space where no one else was focused because there wasn't a market for it yet (the technology hadn't yet been fully invented to enable the application). It was our chance to be first to solve an incredibly big problem. The idea of moving the company in that direction got everyone excited. But what were we supposed to do about the partnership with LG? One thing I knew was that we couldn't do both. That's a trap you can't escape. It's like the old adage that says any football team that has two quarterbacks really has none. We had to make a choice. Should we sign the deal that was guaranteed to profitably grow our company for the next three years, or walk away and start on an entirely new path? What complicated the situation was that we were a public company. That meant we had to make the decision with the best interests of our shareholders in mind—most of whom were focused on next quarter, not next year. That led to some vigorous debates among the leadership team. Was it better to lock in the growth for the short term? Or, would the failure to move in a new direction doom the company in the long run?

What would you have chosen to do? I think it's fair to say that many, if not most, people would have chosen the deal with LG. And I understand why—as the saying goes, "A bird in the hand is worth two in the bush." But I was on the side arguing that if we stayed in a market that was going to commoditize within the next few years, we were not doing what was best for our shareholders. The bird in the hand would become the box that would trap us. We would ultimately provide a greater return for our shareholders if we bet on the next market where we believed our technology would solve a bigger problem and create far more value.

As the deadline to sign with LG loomed, we finally came to our decision: We backed out of the deal at the eleventh hour. We were burning down our box.

That decision wasn't easy for everyone to understand. I remember Ty, one of the leaders of our LED business, coming to my office for three straight days arguing that we needed to sign the deal with LG. Ty was really smart—he had a PhD in materials science and a background working for a major consulting firm and as an entrepreneur. He kept making the point that the LG deal was too good to walk away from. Finally, one day when he showed up to plead his case, I said: "I understand your concerns. But we are betting on lighting. I believe it is in the best interests of the company. We are moving forward." To his credit, Ty nodded and got on board with our march into a bold and bright new future. (Ty would eventually run the lighting business for Cree.)

CREATING THE FUTURE

So you set the box on fire and removed the boundary conditions to create a different future. Now what? How do you get started? At Cree, we started with the question "What do we think the future will look like, five, ten, or twenty years from now?" No limitations— we just imagined how the future would look. Being naïve can sometimes be a superpower when it comes to innovation.

By starting with the end goal and working backward, there was no box to limit our thinking. We worked on many breakthrough innovations during my time at Cree, but none was bigger than the idea that LED lighting could someday replace all conventional lighting technology. The lighting industry affects everyone. Light is a basic human need and artificial light is a fundamental need to enable a civilized society. At the time we were working on this problem, the lighting industry had not changed much since Thomas Edison's discovery of the filament light bulb more than a century earlier. We imagined a future where LED lighting would replace almost all conventional lighting technologies, saving energy and allowing us to bring affordable light to places where it was previously not practical. But this idea was still just in our heads. We needed to tell people what the future looked like, but we struggled to find the words. Then one weekend, Al, a quirky and brilliant marketing person, decided to take matters into his own hands. He decided that we needed a manifesto, a public declaration of our intention to change the world. And the following document was born.

LED LIGHTING MANIFESTO

We declare this as our universal goal: to make energy-wasting, traditional lighting technologies obsolete through the use of energy-efficient, environmentally friendly LED Lighting.
We endeavor to:

1. Reduce the damaging effects of energy inefficiency on our economies and environments

2. Realize energy-efficient lighting products in every country, city, and home

3. Revitalize the lighting industry and release it from its century-old habits

We are the innovators, the pioneers, the dreamers. The ones who see a bright and possible future for humanity. We are the doers, the influencers, the teachers. We are bold and persuasive in communicating the potential and the promise. We are the rebels, the nonconformists, the free spirits. We do not accept the status quo.

We are LED Lighting Revolutionaries.
We proclaim this universal declaration of LED Lighting:

1. All human beings are born into light. Created light is a fundamental and integral part of our productivity, security, and artistic expression as human beings.

2. Creating light consumes energy. The least expensive, most secure, and cleanest energy is the energy that is not used.

3. Proper quantity and quality of light are essential to human perception, performance, and enrichment of life. These should not be sacrificed in the name of energy savings.

4. Poisoning our ground water, lakes, oceans, and fellow humans with toxic mercury is not an acceptable price for energy-efficient lighting.

5. Innovation and creativity can make efficient LED lighting affordable and available to all.

> The LED Lighting Revolution will not come to life on its own; people, corporations, and institutions are the LED Lighting Revolutionaries. Acting alone, working together, and leading others, we accept the mantle of stewardship of the LED Lighting Revolution.
>
> Join us.
>
> The LED Lighting Revolutionaries

That was our big idea. Now that we had publicly stated our intent, all we had to do was invent it, and we could change the world of lighting. Make people's lives a little better. But imagining the future and inventing the technology would prove to be the easiest part.

CONVINCING OTHERS

Once you have created your vision for a different future, how do you convince someone to believe in this new future? For many years, we wanted them to simply believe us. We thought people should see the possibilities of our technology and realize how they would change the world. It was obvious to us, why not to them? We spent many years telling people, hoping they would figure it out, before we realized that our approach was all wrong. If we wanted people to see what was possible, we had to *show them* what it looked like. We had to create a picture of the future by making a convincing and logical argument of what would happen and why. That also meant we had to be willing to put ourselves at risk that we could be wrong.

When we developed the first lighting-class LEDs, we were pretty sure we had something that could change the lighting industry, and maybe even the world. Our first lighting-class LED was four times more efficient than an incandescent light bulb and lasted years longer. And we were just scratching the surface as to what was possible. We knew that theoretically it should be possible to develop an LED that would be even more efficient, up to twenty times better than an incandescent bulb. This was a huge breakthrough, but nobody seemed to care because we hadn't convinced them it was possible. They were stuck in a reality limited by the box. So we set out to show the world what the future would look like.

How do you do that? We created a picture of the future. In this case, a chart that seemed to indicate our future was mathematically inevitable over time. We created a projection or S curve for LED lighting, based on how other technologies had evolved, that showed our technology would continue to improve over the next decade, making LED lighting far better than any other lighting technology available. Keep in mind, we really had no idea how to achieve the results we were projecting ten years into the future, but predicting the future comes with a good deal of risk. That projection gave us a starting point to showing people a different future for lighting.

We used this chart at the first-ever summit on solid-state lighting. Solid-state lighting uses semiconductor LEDs as the source of light instead of filaments, plasma (used in fluorescent lamps), or gas. The executives from all of the major lighting companies were there—but they still believed that LEDs were at best a high-end niche technology. The traditional lighting industry hadn't changed much in over one hundred years, and its leaders believed it would remain the same for many years to come, perhaps because other technologies had previously tried and failed. We were operating outside their box and they tried to shoo us away as just another annoying pest. They either couldn't see the opportunity or didn't want to see it.

MAKE THE FUTURE HAPPEN

We had our picture of the future, and we had made an empirical argument as to why LED was the best technology for lighting. But the market was still not moving. We weren't a big enough company to change the industry on our own. We simply didn't have the resources to influence the behaviors of millions of customers. Yes, we could have continued to be an interesting niche technology. But we wanted to change the world with our innovation—we realized we needed to start an actual revolution, like the one we had described in the LED Lighting Manifesto.

Our idea was that we needed to find a way to make lighting a problem that people cared about. And then to make LED lighting the solution to this problem, a problem people already had, something they were already worried about. At the time, many countries around the world were very concerned about the supply of energy. With the growth in economies around the world, energy prices continued to climb and there was real concern that limited supply would eventually limit economic growth. We knew that lighting accounted for about twenty percent of the world's electricity consumption in buildings. Based on our projections, a global conversion to LED lighting could cut that energy demand in half—cutting global building electricity consumption by ten percent. There was no other technology that was close to making this type of impact in the near term. We had a real problem that the LED Lighting Revolution could solve. And so that became our message.

We started a marketing campaign to spread the word, engaging cities around the world to install LED lighting and show people how they could do things to address the global energy challenges.

And you know what? It worked. It took time, but by making the technology relevant to people, while also connecting them to a larger purpose—they could better themselves and help make the world better—we helped lead a revolution in the kind of light people enjoyed around the world. We helped make the future happen.

While creating the future is a critical step in finding your innovator's spirit, it is often just as important to know what problems to solve and recognize that the customer often doesn't know how to tell you what they really need.

CHAPTER SIX RECAP

Belief: The future doesn't just happen. You have to make it happen.

Behavior: You create the future.

KEY INSIGHTS

There is no box. The box is a choice. The boundary conditions only exist if you allow them to exist.

Sometimes you need to set the box on fire. Don't let yourself get trapped by the status quo. You need courage to acknowledge that you can't keep doing the same things and expect to remain successful.

Create the future. You have to help people see the possibility of something beyond the boundaries of their current reality. And then you need to show them how it solves a problem that they care about.

CHAPTER SEVEN

Solve the Customer's Problem

*"If I'd asked customers what they wanted,
they would have told me, 'A faster horse!'"*

—Henry Ford

YOU'VE PROBABLY HEARD THE PHRASE "the customer is always right." In fact, many consider it a fundamental business principle. The phrase dates back to the early 1900s when innovative retailers like John Wanamaker in Philadelphia and Marshall Field in Chicago began using it.[1] While the phrase apparently was never meant to be taken literally, these retailers adopted it as a strategy to differentiate their stores from their competitors by encouraging their staff to pay special attention to their customers. Treating your customers well is clearly a good business strategy.

But is the customer always right when it comes to innovation? As CEO at Cree, I posed this question to our team, especially those that were new to the organization. I wanted to know whether our new employees believed in conventional wisdom or if they had a sense for the unconventional nature of innovation. Most people assume the customer has to be right—that's what they've always been told—so I enjoyed these moments. This was my opportunity to explain that when it comes to innovation, the customer can't be right, because the customer doesn't know. Don't get me wrong. You need customers. There is no way to create value without them. You can ask what they want, but when it comes to innovation, they can't tell you. Why? Because they can't ask for something they've never seen or experienced before.

Why doesn't the customer know? In the simplest terms, most people are nearsighted. I'm not talking about their eyesight; I'm talking about their imagination. Their idea of what is possible and what they desire is limited by their experiences. They can't possibly ask for something they don't know about—or ask for something they might not even think is possible.

This is why I've always liked Henry Ford's quote about customers wanting faster horses. The idea that they might want a car was simply beyond them. (It's now believed that Ford may have never actually said it, but let's not let that minor detail ruin a great quote.) It highlights the problem of trying to ask your customers what they want when they have no basis of experience in what you are proposing to do. In Ford's case, his insight was that what people really wanted was a fast and affordable means of getting from here to there. Based on the limits of their experience and the world around them, that would lead them to want a faster horse. He understood the problem that needed to be solved.

Consider that Ford grew up on a farm and his dad wanted him to become a farmer. But Ford was far more interested in machinery and learning how machines worked. At a young age, he took apart a watch and taught himself how it ticked. He then began to repair watches for people in town. But his life changed one day when he and his family, as they traveled in their horse-drawn carriage, came across a steam-powered tractor. It blew Ford away. He had seen the future and he wanted to be part of it. Ford eventually left his family's farm and took several jobs where he could learn about steam engines, electricity, and the newest innovation—the gas-powered engine. He became fascinated with the idea that he could build a tractor that could make life easier for farmers like his father when it came to tasks like plowing the field. But he also knew how isolating it was to live on a farm—and how difficult it was to travel to town. He recognized that the problem he had to solve first was getting people like his father to see the value in owning an automobile. As Ford wrote in his autobiography: "I found eventually that people were more interested in something that would travel on the road than in something that would do the work on the farms. In fact, I doubt that the light farm tractor could have been introduced on the farm had not the farmer had his eyes opened slowly but surely by the automobile."[2]

As Ford began to build his first car, other early motorcars already existed around the country. But when he finished his first "gasoline buggy" in 1895, it became the first car to be driven on the streets of Detroit. He received much fanfare for his invention—which he sold for $200. It was just a prototype and he had many ideas about how to improve it. At the time, he was working for the Detroit Edison

Company, but his supervisor didn't approve of him working on his invention on the side. He offered Ford a promotion—but only if he gave up his side hustle of building cars. To Ford, the choice was easy: He chose his automobile—even though he had no money and a family to support. The stakes were even higher because, as he wrote: "There was no 'demand' for automobiles—there never is for a new article. At first the 'horseless carriage' was considered merely a freak notion and many wise people explained with particularity why it could never be more than a toy. No man of money even thought of it as a commercial possibility. . . . In the beginning there was hardly anyone who sensed that the automobile could be a large factor in industry." In other words, the public didn't yet understand the true value of this invention.

But Ford was undeterred. Even after a failed stint with the Detroit Automobile Company (which later became Cadillac), where he clashed with the management team who wanted to make expensive custom cars to order like other emerging car companies did, Ford pursued his vision for making a "universal car for the multitudes" by forming his own company, the Ford Motor Company, in 1903. It was there that he perfected his designs and, just as important, learned how to mass-produce quality automobiles like his famous Model T at reasonable prices. "Making 'to order' instead of making in volume is, I suppose, a habit, a tradition, that has descended from the old handicraft days," Ford wrote. "But if you manufacture at the very highest quality and sell at the very lowest price, you will be meeting a demand which is so large that it may be called universal." Put another way, Ford had figured out the real problem to solve for his customers, even if they hadn't realized it for themselves. He was making the kinds of cars they could afford, and without having to make trade-offs in terms of quality or service. Thanks to Ford's innovator's spirit, he saw what his customers could not. He then laid the groundwork for the world's first mass-produced automobiles—and he changed the world forever as a result.

FINDING THE PROBLEM TO SOLVE

If the customer doesn't know, how do you go about figuring out the problem they need solved? Easy, you ask your customers a lot of questions. And then you find new ways to connect the dots. But don't expect them to tell you what to do.

Imagine the following scene at a local home improvement store. Dan works at the store. Yet he is not your ordinary retail employee. Dan is a recently retired professor of innovation from a local college. After retiring, he was spending a little too much time around the house providing his wife of many years with advice that she didn't ask for. So she suggested he find something to do with himself and he ended up with a job helping people in the tool aisle. One day at his new job, Dan approaches a customer who is standing in the tool section looking a bit confused by all of the different products available. Dan asks him if he needs any help. The customer turns to Dan and says, "I need a quarter-inch drill bit."

Dan smiles and asks, "Why do you want the drill bit?"

"Because I need to create a quarter-inch hole," the customer responds.[3]

Dan smiles again and asks, "Why do you want a quarter-inch hole?"

The customer says he wants to put a screw in the wall to hold a bracket. Dan smiles and asks, "Why do you want to hang a bracket?"

The customer starts to get a bit annoyed at this point. *What is it with this clerk?* he thinks. Out loud, he says, "I need the bracket to hold a shelf."

Dan smiles and asks, "Why do you want a shelf?"

Now the customer is pretty steamed. *Just give me what I want*, he thinks. But in response to Dan's question, he says he needs the shelf to hold some books.

"Aha!" Dan exclaims. "Now I understand the problem you're trying to solve. Here is the drill bit you should buy."

What Dan was really thinking at the end of the conversation was that if the customer simply bought e-books, they wouldn't need a shelf at all. But he had been reminded by his boss that his job depended on people actually buying things in the store, so he kept this last thought to himself.

What's the point of the story? No, it's not that retired innovation professors shouldn't work at home improvement stores. Rather, it's to point out that while the customer often doesn't know how to tell you what they want, if you listen carefully, they can describe the problem that needs to be solved. The key to innovation lies in finding a way to solve their problem.

But how do you listen to your customers? Isn't that simply market research? If traditional market research could have identified the innovative idea, someone else would already be doing it. In a 1995 interview later posted on YouTube, Steve Jobs, replying to a question about the role that market research played in the early days of Apple, said:

> The problem is that market research can tell you what your customers think of something you show them, or it can tell you what your customers want as an incremental improvement on what you have, but very rarely can your

customers predict something that they don't even quite know they want yet. As an example, no market research could have led to the development of the Macintosh or the personal computer in the first place. So there are these non-incremental jumps that need to take place where it's very difficult for market research to really contribute much in the early phases of thinking about what those should be.[4]

Similarly, when Jobs was asked how much market research was done in developing the iPad, he replied: "None. It's not for consumers to know what they want."[5]

In the YouTube video, Jobs does go on to say that it can be valuable to check your instincts with the market after you have a product in hand—at which point they might begin to see the value of it. The point is that you can't ask your customers what to do when it comes to innovation; you need to go do it first, then show them and see how they react.

A word of caution: Taking this idea out of context can be dangerous to your success. This concept is not an excuse to ignore your customers and do what you want. There's a huge difference between not asking your customers what to do and ignoring their needs and problems. The idea is to ask the right questions to focus on the problem your customers don't know they have, and then find a new solution. In the end, it's still about creating value for the customer.

OPENING UP NEW OPPORTUNITIES

Finding ways to innovate and solve problems no one else is tackling can open all kinds of new opportunities, what you might call "blue oceans." That's a term coined by business professors W. Chan Kim and Renée Mauborgne in their best-selling book *Blue Ocean Strategy*. Kim and Mauborgne write about how many companies operate in "red oceans," where they face stiff competition, rather than finding ways to move into competition-free "blue oceans." And to do that, they argue, companies need to think beyond making incremental improvements to the existing status quo and do something innovative instead. "Our studies revealed that [innovation] is about redefining the problem an industry focuses on rather than finding solutions to existing problems," they write.

One great example of a business that found a blue ocean is the Canadian-based performance troupe Cirque du Soleil. If you've never been to one of their performances, you're missing out. It's a true spectacle that mixes incredibly athletic aerial stunts—people literally fly through the air—with storylines and even some comedy. Cirque du Soleil created "a new form of entertainment that offers the fun and thrill of the circus with the intellectual sophistication of the theater."[6] It's something utterly unique—something I didn't fully appreciate until I had a chance to visit their company headquarters in Montreal, Canada, several years ago. The place mixed a giant gymnasium where performers practiced breathtaking new acts with an amazing costume design factory where they were inventing new kinds of costumes that could keep up with the acts of the performers.

At last official count, Cirque du Soleil shows have been seen by more than 150 million people in some three hundred cities around the world. It has become a cultural phenomenon at a time when attendance at more traditional circuses has fallen off dramatically. In fact, attendance became so bad at the iconic Ringling Bros. and Barnum & Bailey Circus—formerly known as "the Greatest Show on Earth"—that it was forced to shut down after 146 years, with its last live performance coming in 2017.[7] What did Cirque du Soleil realize that the traditional circus folks missed? They didn't rely on what customers were asking for, and instead they solved an entertainment problem.

Consider what it might have been like in 1984 if you were the founders of Cirque du Soleil. Basically, you have come up with a new invention—a combination of high-flying circus acts mixed with theater. How do you think that would have market-tested—especially at a time when competition for people's entertainment dollars had become increasingly fierce? Would theatergoers have suggested adding circus acts? And what if you asked kids—the customers who normally loved the circus—what they wanted? Do you think they would have said they wished the circus were more artsy and theatrical? No chance. There was no basis for audiences to even imagine this concept was possible.

What's interesting is that around the time that Cirque du Soleil made its debut, traditional circuses were asking their customers what they wanted. And they gave them more of what they asked for. They tried to "secure more famous clowns and lion tamers, a strategy that raised a circus's cost structure without substantially altering the circus experience. The result was rising costs without rising revenues, and a downward spiral of overall circus demand."[8] Put another way, the more the circuses listened to what their customers said they wanted, the worse off they became. The circus operators didn't know how to ask questions to really understand the problem that needed to be solved.

Then Cirque du Soleil came around. Its founders decided to approach the problem in a completely different way. They were going to solve the problem of providing customers with entertainment they were willing to pay for by rethinking the entire equation. It was clearly not an accident that their first performance was titled "We Reinvent the Circus." As the authors of *Blue Ocean Strategy* frame the situation:

> Instead of following the conventional logic of outpacing the competition by offering a better solution to the given problem—creating a circus with even greater fun and thrills—it sought to offer people the fun and thrill of the circus and the intellectual sophistication and artistic richness of the theater at the same time; hence, it redefined the problem itself. By breaking the market boundaries of theater and circus, Cirque du Soleil gained a new understanding not only of circus customers but also of circus non customers: adult theater customers. This led to a whole new circus concept.[9]

Cirque du Soleil reportedly reached a similar revenue scale in its first twenty years that took Ringling Bros. and Barnum & Bailey a hundred years to achieve—largely thanks to connecting the dots in a new and different way that created a solution that the customer valued but could never have imagined.

We've seen other recent examples like this as well. Think about how companies like Uber and Lyft have radically upended the traditional taxi industry, which has been a staple of American life ever since cars were invented. Can you imagine conducting early market research for Uber? How do you think you'd react if someone suggested that you could request a car using your phone, hop into some random stranger's personal car, and then never give them cash or your credit card? It sounds more like a hitchhiking service than a taxi alternative. Or, flipping that around, how many people would have volunteered to drive for such a service? And let's not forget the fact that taxi drivers essentially had monopolies in the form of licenses or "medallions" in many cities. The company would have to find a way around those regulations—plus convince customers to pay more than they were used to paying for a regular taxi.[10] Was the ability to call a car with your phone worth a premium? Given all of that, do you think you would have predicted the huge demand on both sides of this equation that has led to the creation of an entire new market category and in the process has disrupted both the taxi and rental car industries?

Or what about the company Airbnb, where you can also use your phone to rent a room or even a whole house—with the added wrinkle that someone probably lives there. It was started in San Francisco by a couple of designers who capitalized on surges of visitors from around the world by renting out a room in their apartment for $80 a night.[11] They realized that there could be a huge market for others to do the same thing. If they asked you, you might have thought, *Wait, you want me to go sleep in some stranger's house instead of a hotel? I don't think so.* But the founders of Airbnb understood the problem they could solve: give travelers access to discounted lodging that, in some cases, was nicer than any hotel. Not only that, they also gave homeowners and renters the chance to turn their rooms and homes into a chance to earn some extra money. But if they had asked you, would you have predicted that this would become a multibillion-dollar global innovation? I'm not sure I would have. Which is again the key point here, that people don't know what to ask for—especially when it comes to innovation. In the case of Uber, Lyft, and Airbnb, they used technology to create a market that nobody knew they wanted until they could experience it. Sometimes you just have to do it and then show them what it looks like.

SHOWING THEM WHAT IT LOOKS LIKE

There are going to be times as an innovator when you can get too far out in front of your customers—meaning that they can't recognize the value of what you've created. What do you do then? I think you try several times to convince them of the future, but at some point, you just have to show them what it looks like.

This happened to us at Cree. In the company's early days—well before anyone thought about making LED lighting—we were a semiconductor materials company. We made the thing that went inside the thing that went into the product you could actually buy. In our case, we were an LED chip company. We made blue LED chips that we sold to LED packaging companies, who then sold the packaged LEDs to consumer electronics companies, automakers, and sign companies. These LED chips were used in what we called low-power applications, like the LED indicator in the switch on your computer monitor that tells you when the power is on. Then a day came when we heard that a company called Lumileds was developing large, high-power LED blue chips for white LEDs that were ten to twenty times brighter than our blue chips. They were an LED packager that also made their own chips. Lumileds was a joint venture between Philips Lighting and the division of Hewlett-Packard where I had started my career—these were my former colleagues, friends, and family—my brother Mark was Lumileds's head of sales and marketing.

This sounded like an interesting challenge to our scientists, so they began developing our own high-power LED chip. They eventually created a blue chip that was much brighter than what Lumileds had demonstrated. We thought, *This is awesome!* We had found a way to enable the holy grail of LED applications—to use LEDs for lighting. But, at the time, we were just the "blue LED" chip company. We needed to sell our chip to packaging companies so they could make these new high-power LEDs for lighting and sell them to the market.

We approached Lumileds, and they agreed to test our new blue chip in their package. After running some tests, they said it worked great—better than their own chip. I remember thinking, *Great! We just landed a new customer.* But they weren't interested in buying our chips. They told us they were going to stick with their own chips, even if they weren't as bright. We were confused. We had just made something that was twice as good as theirs, but they weren't interested. It was a classic case of NIH (not-invented-here) syndrome. OK, we said, we'll shop it around to the LED packagers who were already buying our low-power blue chips. Surely somebody would want to run with this idea. But every potential packaging customer we approached responded the same way: They thought our new LED chip was great, but they didn't want to buy it. "Why?" we asked. "Because our customers aren't asking for it," they all told us.

Obviously, this frustrated us. We had a new class of blue LED chip that could transform an entire new industry. But the companies who could use these chips didn't want to buy them. They didn't see the future because their customers couldn't see the future. They also didn't have the expertise to utilize the technology. We knew it was an incredible invention, but what could we do? We were an LED chip company, not a packager. In the end, we decided that we had no choice but to do it ourselves. We were going to package our own chips and make the first "lighting class" white LEDs. If our packaging customers couldn't recognize the opportunity in front of them, then we needed to go directly to the lighting companies—which meant we would be indirectly competing with our existing customers. This wasn't an easy decision to make and not one to be taken lightly. Our argument was that we're not competing if you don't make these types of products—and they didn't. But it still made many of our existing chip customers nervous, which led to a number of uncomfortable conversations over the next several years. But it was the right thing to do. We knew we had the keys to creating an LED-based lighting industry, and it wasn't going to happen by waiting around and hoping the customers figured out how to ask for something they couldn't imagine was possible.

So off we went and developed our own high-power packaged LED—the Cree XLamp. It was the world's first lighting-class LED. We built a production line and hired a few salespeople to focus on selling these products to customers that we had never sold to before. We had some initial success in winning a few contracts for new designs in flashlights and the emergency lights that go on top of police cars, but we had no luck with the lighting companies. We spent a couple of years making our pitch to the large lighting-fixture manufacturers, telling them how they could create great products using our LEDs—and how there would be no more light bulbs to change. The LEDs were not only really bright, but they also lasted forever (we quoted one hundred thousand hours, which is more than ten years if the lights are on continuously) and used a fraction of the energy. We thought we had a slam dunk on our hands. How could they say no?

But they did. None of the major lighting customers were interested. And so again, we asked, "Why not?" In what seemed like déjà vu, we again heard, "Because our customers aren't asking for it. They're happy with what they have." We were back to square one. We had developed a breakthrough LED that could completely change the lighting industry. But nobody wanted to use these LEDs to develop lighting products because their customers weren't asking for them. It was incredibly frustrating. We had a product that could change the world, and again, no one seemed to see its potential except us.

Yet again, we were forced into a reckoning: What should we do? Were we crazy enough to become an actual lighting company—to compete against yet another set of potential customers by selling directly to the end customer? Yes, it turned out, we were. The process began when Neal Hunter, who was running the LED company LLF at the time, approached me and made the argument that Cree and LLF could form an effective partnership that could take on the status quo in the lighting business. After we discussed the idea, I realized that LLF could become the marketing strategy for LED lighting that we had been missing. If we could prove to the end customers that LED technology had real value in lighting, they would start asking all of their suppliers for it. If we proved LED lighting was real, the lighting industry would have to respond. Buying LLF was our rabbit strategy, to run out in front on the industry big dogs and get them to chase the rabbit. We knew we had the chance to do something monumental—to disrupt an entire industry, maybe even the world. So we did. And it worked.

Cree showed the world what LED lighting could do, and once customers knew what was possible, they started asking for it. I was often asked if this idea of competing with our LED customers was a bad strategy. My response was that if we did nothing, we would have incredible market share for a product that had no demand. Alternatively, we could enable LED lighting and have a smaller share of a huge market. The choice seemed obvious to me. This was the innovator's spirit in action.

There are big opportunities waiting for you if you can solve the problems your customers don't know they have. There are potentially even bigger blue oceans waiting for you if you pursue the things that other people tell you can't be done.

CHAPTER SEVEN RECAP

Belief: People can't ask for something they don't know is possible.

Behavior: Solve the customer's problem.

KEY INSIGHTS

The customer doesn't know. They can't relate to something they've never seen or experienced before.

Listen carefully. The customer can't tell you what to do, but if you listen carefully, they can describe the problem that needs to be solved.

Show them. You can try to convince people of the future, but at some point, you just have to show them what it looks like.

CHAPTER EIGHT

Do What They Say You Can't

"When someone tells you it can't be done, it's more a reflection of their limitations, not yours."

—Unknown

HAVE YOU EVER HAD SOMEONE in your life tell you something simply couldn't be done—maybe even that whatever you were thinking of doing was "impossible"? What did you do? Did you give up? Did you argue that you could? Or did you smile to yourself, say thank you, and then set out to prove them wrong? This was actually a common occurrence at Cree—so common, in fact, that it became an integral part of our approach to innovation. Why did I say thank you?

(To be clear, I didn't say it out loud, but I was thinking it.) Because when someone says you can't do something, they are actually telling you what you should do—it's an opportunity to go beyond what your rivals or competition believes they are capable of. They are telling you which problem you can solve to create an innovation.

This approach was especially true in our lighting business. We had great technology that we believed would enable LED lighting, but we didn't know anything about the market. As you'll recall from the previous chapter, we had always thought of Cree as a semiconductor or components company—not a provider of lighting systems. We had discussed at one point whether we should consider developing lighting products. But we had decided that we didn't know enough to get into that business. And then we bought the LED lighting company LLF—which meant we were now selling the world's first commercially viable LED lighting fixture.

To put this innovation in perspective, compact fluorescent lighting (CFL) had emerged several decades earlier as the longer-lasting, energy-saving replacement for the incandescent bulb. Unfortunately, those lights also had a problem. They required the customer to compromise. They didn't emit the warm, incandescent-like light customers were used to. They also didn't work with dimmers and they took a while to warm up and get to full brightness. While most people were interested in saving energy, they were not willing to sacrifice functionality. As a result, most customers avoided them and the market for CFLs never fully developed. The LLF product was different. It was a no-compromise way to save energy and save money. We knew that for LED lighting to become mainstream, we had to make a product that performed every bit as well as the lights they were replacing—delivering a bright and warm light that was also long lasting and efficient. The product needed to be so good that nobody could tell it wasn't an incandescent.

We had some initial success with the LLF (now Cree) $99 LED downlights in the hospitality industry. Restaurants and hotels, establishments that kept their lights on twenty-four hours a day and yet also needed the light quality of an incandescent, became the early adopters of our lights. With the success of the downlights, we garnered the attention of lighting designers who were being asked by their clients why they couldn't use LEDs in other applications. Retail customers saw our success in hospitality and started asking designers if they could use LED technology to replace the halogen spot lamps that were used in the track lights common in most stores. These customers knew the halogen lamps required frequent replacement, used a lot of energy, and were expensive. Despite our success with downlights, lighting design professionals believed that making an LED light capable of replacing these special lamps wasn't possible. They said it couldn't be done, which motivated our R&D team to prove them wrong and develop an LED alternative.

We decided to demo our new LED spot lamps at the annual lighting industry trade show in New York City, where we used them to illuminate our booth. When skeptical designers stopped by, they chided us for still using halogen bulbs to light up our booth when we were touting that we had made advances with our LED products. "You have it wrong," we told them, "those are LED lamps." They shook their heads; they didn't believe us. "Look," we said, "come back to the booth after the show ends and we'll prove it to you." Once the show ended and most everyone had cleared out of the convention center, we let the designers climb a ladder and inspect the LED lamps firsthand so they could see it for themselves. They were shocked. They couldn't believe we had done what they thought wasn't possible. From that moment forward, designers started to embrace the possibility of LED lighting.

Another challenge of what couldn't be done came from within our own lighting team. Among the many talented engineers on our team, some had previously worked at other lighting companies and were "lighting experts," which wasn't always a benefit. While they believed that LED could do some great things and had been instrumental in the success of our LED downlight, they thought it could never replace the de facto standard of the commercial lighting world: the linear fluorescent light tube. These two-by-two or two-by-four-foot-long fixtures were cheap and efficient and pervasive in almost every office building around the world. Some of our engineers believed LEDs could never hope to compete with let alone replace fluorescent light tubes. Yet again, our LED scientists saw this challenge as an opportunity to introduce an LED product into the market to prove their "lighting expert" coworkers wrong. And they did. Our product was not only more efficient than the fluorescent alternative, it had great color quality, which was something that fluorescent couldn't do. By doing what even some of our colleagues said we couldn't do, we created another new market for LED lighting—and the industry was forced to play catch-up once again.

As our lighting business grew, we started to get more attention from the big industry players—and not always the good kind. We were challenging their market position and role in the industry. They had been telling customers what to buy and what was possible for decades, and we were now challenging those assumptions. LED lights already had the benefit of saving energy, but we also developed a way to guarantee cost savings with the first-ever five-year warranty for our LED lights—which was unheard of in the industry. Keep in mind, at that time everyone expected lights to regularly burn out and need to be replaced.

At one point, George, the general manager of a division of a large U.S. lighting company, came to visit Cree. These meetings were always a bit awkward. On one hand, we were trying to sell LEDs to the lighting companies. And on the other hand, we kept disrupting the status quo by doing things with LEDs that weren't supposed to be possible. We were discussing a variety of topics with George when he said, "We can see that you're having some success with your $100 downlight in niche commercial markets, but LED will never be relevant in the high-volume markets like residential. The product is simply too expensive."

I was used to being told what we couldn't do at this point, so I didn't overreact. I listened to George go on for a few minutes and then I said, "I agree that LED downlights are more expensive than traditional downlights. What would you think they'd need to cost to be relevant in those high-volume applications?"

George smiled and said, "You would have to be able to sell your downlight for less than $50 at retail." I agreed that this would be a difficult challenge and the conversation shifted to other topics. But I knew what we needed to do. He had just told us what it would take to sell direct to consumers. This conversation brought me back to that time I visited the White House, where Secretary Chu challenged me with the notion that LEDs would not be viable until they paid for themselves. Guess what happened next? A few weeks later I sat down with Tony, one of the LLF cofounders, in his office in Hong Kong and gave him the challenge of creating a cheaper version of our downlight that we could sell for less than $50. As I described the problem that day, he stood at the white board and sketched out the initial concept for how we would make our new low-cost downlight a reality. And I knew we had a product that would pay for itself in only a few years.

Several months later, in an unrelated meeting with the merchant at one of the major home improvement retailers, we asked him if their customers would be interested in our downlights if they could buy them for under $50. The buyer gave us an enthusiastic response, not knowing that a prototype already existed. After several months and more hard work by our engineers, we soon had a product that was on the shelves retailing for $49.95—and reset industry and consumer expectations around LED lighting. It was now a technology that anyone could buy and get the benefit of saving energy.

In each of these cases, we responded to the challenges of the naysayers by turning their doubts into incredible opportunities to innovate. But keep in mind, when opportunity knocks, you have to answer the door. You don't pick these moments; these moments or opportunities choose you. After only a few years in the LED lighting business and doing what they said we couldn't, we had gone from a small start-up that nobody believed in to a leader in the lighting business that was challenging hundred-year-old assumptions.

MAKING THE IMPOSSIBLE POSSIBLE

Can you make a rock fly? Of course you can, you just throw it into the air, right? But can you make it really fly—like a bird or a plane—where the rock is able to maintain flight over an extended distance? The answer seems obvious. Almost anyone will tell you a rock can't fly, because it has no capability of lift, which is required for flight. It's just something you can't do. Or is it?

When I was a college student in the late 1980s, I had a professor named Susan Riedel, who had studied aeronautics at MIT before coming to Marquette University. At the time, she was finishing her PhD and teaching a class on computer engineering. She had a way of helping students see engineering problems from a practical perspective. One day, while trying to motivate us to solve a really difficult problem, she said: "It's like the helicopter, which is basically a rock flying through the air. It has no inherent aeronautical properties. But somebody figured out how to strap a motor on it and make it fly." Since that day, I've realized that anything is possible. I've also been curious about who did what others said can't be done and made a rock fly.

One of those innovators was Igor Sikorsky, who was born in Kiev, Ukraine, in 1889. Even at a young age, he was fascinated with the idea of flight. He was especially inspired by the drawings of Leonardo da Vinci's "helical airscrew" and the concept of a helicopter-like vessel in Jules Verne's book *Robur the Conqueror*. He began experimenting with electric motors and chemistry in his room—where he made such a mess that the family maid apparently refused to enter it. Sikorsky's passion for flying was stoked to a new level in 1908 when he joined his father on a trip to France where Orville Wright was demonstrating his and his brother's plane. It was then that he became convinced that "a practical helicopter could be produced."[1]

While he threw himself into the work of building a prototype, he never succeeded in getting his contraption to lift off the ground; the engines he had at his disposal weren't powerful enough. In 1909 Sikorsky returned to Paris, the hub of the aviation world at that time. He introduced himself to many of the leading aviators of the era, including Captain Ferdinand Ferber, a pioneering glider. When Sikorsky told Ferber about his idea of a machine that could take off vertically, Ferber shook his head. "Do not waste your time on a helicopter," Ferber told Sikorsky. "The airplane will be far more valuable." He added, "To invent a flying machine is nothing; to build it is little; to make it fly is everything."[2] Those words became a motto that stuck with Sikorsky for the rest of his career.

It seemed like anyone who Sikorsky told about his project was cynical about its success. As one of Sikorsky's biographers puts it: "Few aviators knew anything about such a revolutionary device, so their advice was limited by their ignorance." Undeterred, he kept experimenting for the next two years with more powerful engines—nearly killing himself several times in the process. "I learned in those first two years the immense difficulty of pioneering in the helicopter field as well as my own vast ignorance," he wrote.

As a way to further educate himself on the subject of aeronautics, Sikorsky changed course and began building an airplane, the S-1. What he didn't realize at the time was that making airplanes would consume the next thirty years of his life, where he would team up with icons of the air like Charles Lindbergh to build some of the sturdiest planes of the era.

Sikorsky fled Russia's revolution in 1919 and eventually boarded a steamship that brought him to America, where he wanted to follow in the footsteps of other inventors like Edison and Ford. Sikorsky eventually started his own aircraft manufacturing company, Sikorsky Aero Engineering Corporation, with funding from the composer and pianist Sergei Rachmaninoff.[3] It was there that Sikorsky led the pioneering efforts to build planes that could land on water, so-called flying boats, because the United States did not yet have any kind of airport infrastructure. But by the 1930s, Sikorsky had become part of a consortium of companies called United Technologies. And as the need for flying boats waned, the management at the company threatened to close the Sikorsky plant.

That was when Sikorsky proposed dusting off his earlier designs for a helicopter—something he said would "prove to be a unique instrument in the saving of human lives."[4] At the time, several other inventors were at work trying to solve the conundrum of vertical flight. Even Nikola Tesla filed a patent for his helicopter design. But no one had yet succeeded in creating a machine that could reliably take off, fly, and then land. In fact, as Sikorsky wrote, "The helicopter at that time was one of the impossibilities. Many people considered that no helicopter with real control characteristics could ever be constructed. Other pessimists said that even if you did build a helicopter, no one would need it."[5]

But Sikorsky saw that as his opportunity. He said he would "design a new type of flying machine without knowing how to design it, then build it without knowing how to build it, and then try to test-fly it without ever having flown a helicopter before."[6]

That's exactly what he did when, on September 14, 1939, he strapped himself into his VS-300, a machine made up of welded pipes topped with a three-bladed rotor, and lifted into the air. It was later described by one observer as "a farmer's windmill flying by."[7] With further modifications, Sikorsky's machine could hover, fly backward and forward and side to side, and then land back where it started. It was a flying machine like no other.

Even then, the doubters remained: What practical use was such a machine? Of course, the helicopter would prove to have many uses. It could be put to humanitarian uses like dropping off emergency aid to disaster victims, for example, and there were the obvious military applications as well. But Sikorsky understood the real problem his helicopter solved: It could go places other aircraft couldn't. As he put it: "What kind of machine can give you unlimited freedom of transportation?"[8] And while others told him that wasn't possible, he always knew it was.

WHEN OPPORTUNITY KNOCKS

It turns out that history is full of innovators who turned the scorn of the skeptics and cynics into the motivation to do something that had never been done before. These innovators realized that not only were the skeptics wrong, but opportunity was also knocking.

Consider how Clarence Birdseye turned a hunting trip to Newfoundland—where he learned how the indigenous Inuit "quick-froze" their game to help ensure its flavor—into his idea for frozen food. While people told him that the American consumer would never buy frozen meat or vegetables, Birdseye persisted in experimenting with his own quick-freeze technology until he got it right in 1924.[9] He later sold his patents to General Foods Corporation, who not only made Birdseye a millionaire, but also launched a national marketing campaign to show how tasty Birdseye "frosted foods" really were. Our grocery stores have never been the same because Birdseye recognized an opportunity and didn't listen to the doubters, instead creating an entire category of food that the skeptics said nobody wanted.

In the 1950s, the management at television studios didn't think a show featuring a feisty redheaded comedian named Lucille Ball and her husband, a Cuban man named Desi Arnaz, would work. So Ball and Arnaz created a pilot with their own money for a show they called *I Love Lucy*. Even then, the management types at the studios told them the show would have to be shot in New York using blurry camera technology called kinescopes to be compatible with the images American TVs were capable of showing at the time. But Ball and Arnaz—whose company was called Desilu—were looking further into the future than that. They wanted to shoot their show in Hollywood using the same kind of film the movie sets used—which was much more expensive than the old technology. Still facing roadblocks from the TV studios (this was a time long before online streaming or YouTube), Ball and Arnaz agreed to take a pay cut to make the show, in return for keeping ownership rights to their show—which became incredibly valuable. Ball and Arnaz did what the experts said you couldn't do and created one of the most watched shows on TV. The success of the show—and how it was filmed—transformed the way TV shows were created from that point on.[10]

And think about how we take conveniences like free two-day or even one-day shipping for granted these days. None of that would have been possible if not for the determination of a man named Fred Smith to prove the naysayers wrong. In the 1960s as a student at Yale University, Smith wrote a term paper for an economics class about the feasibility of an overnight delivery business. Smith had seen the future and had outlined a thorough plan for making such a novel service a possibility. Only, when he got his paper back from the professor, he was stunned: He had gotten a C. The professor reportedly added the following note to Smith's paper: "The concept is interesting and well-formed, but in order to earn better than a 'C,' the idea must be feasible."

But Smith never gave up on his vision. After serving in the Vietnam War, he went back to work on his idea of creating an integrated air and ground delivery system based on a hub-and-spoke framework. Federal Express, or FedEx, began operating in 1973 with a total of fourteen jets servicing twenty-five cities. While the company lost a lot of money early on—at one point it was bleeding around $1 million a month—Smith kept at it. Then, helped by a popular marketing campaign that featured the tagline "FedEx—when it absolutely, positively has to be there overnight," the company went public in 1980 and continued to grow from there.[11] Today, FedEx is the largest overnight shipper in the world—in spite of a college professor who didn't think it was feasible. When the experts say you can't, it is often a signal that you have found a problem worth solving. But also keep in mind, you have to do more than realize that opportunity is knocking, you have to answer the door and do something about it.

CONFRONTING THE INNOVATOR'S DILEMMA

While some people may tell you it can't be done, others will try to convince you that it shouldn't be done. This often is presented as sage advice, but it's the same trap. Assume for a minute that you are a consultant working for a company that makes traditional incandescent light bulbs. Then, one day, your client tells you they've invented a light bulb that never burns out. What do you advise them to do with it?

You might be surprised to learn that this was an actual interview question that a large consulting firm used in the years before the LED light bulb was invented. What answer do you think they were looking for? The consultants wanted to hear that you would advise your client to shelve the idea and not tell anyone. Why? Because it would severely hurt and possibly kill their existing business.

You can imagine how this same question could be posed to companies in other industries as well. If you invented a printer that never needed to refill the ink, for example, what would you do? It would kill the printer ink cartridge business model. Or what if you invented tires that lasted for a hundred thousand miles instead of twenty thousand? You would effectively reduce the demand for tires by eighty percent, which can't be good for the tire business. The conventional answer that most companies have embraced throughout history is don't tell anyone. Their thinking is you do whatever it takes to protect the business you have. You tell innovators to stop innovating because it's too dangerous to the existing business—the business that pays the bills—and if something changes, we might all lose our jobs.

What's your reaction to that strategy? This was a highly regarded and expensive consulting firm recommending this approach, but is it really good advice? No, it's not. Innovation doesn't stop. You're simply delaying the inevitable and giving a competitor the chance to catch up and move ahead. While you might be able to preserve the status quo in the short term, you're dooming yourself for the long run. I saw this firsthand as the "big three" global light bulb companies pretended that, despite the invention of the LED and our projections that it would change the world, their business would not change. Maybe they believed the technology wasn't real, or maybe they had hired those same consultants I mentioned earlier. I remember being pulled aside at a conference by one lighting CEO who told me to slow down, this trend could be bad for business. He said they had a lot of money invested in factories making light bulbs and CFLs. If an LED bulb came out that lasted for ten years, it would kill their business. So they waited and we kept going. When the "big three" finally realized the market was changing without them, they were too late. Their legacy business started to shrink and today those businesses are a fraction of what they once were. This is the *innovator's dilemma*, a term popularized by Clayton Christensen in his book of the same name. As President Barack Obama said: "Sticking your head in the sand might make you feel safer, but it's not going to protect you from the coming storm."

The classic example of this dynamic in action is Kodak. It wasn't that long ago that Kodak was one of the most successful companies in America. If you had a camera, you probably used Kodak film to snap your photos. At one time, Kodak film was used by more than eighty percent of the market in the United States—and about fifty percent globally.[12] Innovator George Eastman from Rochester, New York, filed his first patent for a photographic plate in 1877. Later, he also patented the first camera to use film in rolls instead of plates[13]—a technology that spurred him to create the company Eastman Kodak in 1888.[14]

Nearly a century later, in 1975, a twenty-four-year-old Kodak engineer named Steve Sasson created the first digital camera. The technology was rudimentary by today's standards—its photos were just 0.01 megapixels—which is a fraction of what our smartphones are capable of today.[15] Nevertheless, it was a breakthrough technology. But what did this device represent to Kodak? When Sasson demonstrated his prototype to Kodak's management team and showed them how he could take instantaneous photos and then project them on a screen, he heard crickets. "They were convinced that no one would ever want to look at their pictures on a television set," Sasson told a *New York Times* reporter. "Print had been with us for over one hundred years, no one was complaining about prints, they were very inexpensive, and so why would anyone want to look at their picture on a television set?"[16] What did Kodak's management team do? They told Sasson he couldn't talk to anyone outside of the company about his prototype. They were concerned that it would cannibalize the company's extremely profitable and entrenched film business. "Every digital camera that was sold took away from a film camera and we knew how much money we made on film," Sasson said. "That was the argument. Of course, the problem is pretty soon you won't be able to sell film—and that was my position."[17] But the management team wasn't ready to confront the future. So it put the digital camera technology in a closet and shut the door.

Twenty years later, Kodak finally introduced its first digital camera to the market, but by then the company had been outflanked by the competition—and film was falling out of favor. In 2006 Kodak discontinued Kodachrome, the cash-cow product it had been producing for seventy-four years. Then, the company essentially collapsed in 2012 when it declared bankruptcy—and some sixty thousand people lost their jobs.[18] While the company has reinvented itself somewhat based on leveraging the licensing fees it earns from its patents, it's far from the powerhouse it once was—all because the company was more interested in protecting what it had rather than investing in the future. As a *Forbes* columnist framed it: "It is not that Kodak had failed to imagine a new future. It had failed to capitalize on the imagination and inventiveness of its scientists."[19]

The point is that innovation is going to happen and even the most successful business will be forced to change. The key is to seize the opportunity before it seizes your business. You need to be willing to do what your own people might tell you is impossible, even if it seems like you might fail as a result. But one of the keys to uncovering your innovator's spirit is to embrace the idea that failure is the fuel of innovation.

CHAPTER EIGHT RECAP

Belief: When someone says you can't, you probably should.

Behavior: Do what they say you can't.

KEY INSIGHTS

When opportunity knocks, you have to answer the door. When someone says it can't be done, you have found a problem worth solving.

Make the impossible, possible. Innovation is doing what others tell you is impossible.

Seize the opportunity before it seizes you. Change is constant. Change is opportunity. Innovation is going to happen whether you choose to participate or not.

CHAPTER NINE

Be Unafraid
of Failure

"Those who dare to fail miserably can achieve greatly."
—John F. Kennedy

BUILDING OUR TEAM WAS A critical and never-ending activity. Whether the position was a direct report of mine or someone who would become part of the larger Cree team, I became more and more focused on trying to identify who might best fit in our innovation-driven culture. I looked for a number of different things as I tried to understand what beliefs drove each person's behaviors. Members of my team would often ask: "What is the most important quality you're looking for?" My answer was that it was never just one thing; it was a combination of things. That said, I started with looking for people who were *unafraid of failure—yet unwilling to fail.* In Chapter Four, I talked about the concept of finding a way to win, which is the same principle as being unwilling to fail. But what does it mean to be unafraid of failure? How do you not let your fear of failure and desire to manage risk keep you from chasing an amazing opportunity?

Early in my career at Cree, I received a frantic call from Norbert Hiller, who was running the LED business at Siemens, a large German industrial company. Norbert was one of our LED chip customers and he needed to talk with me right away.

Before I continue with the story, let me give you some background. A few months prior to this call, we had given Siemens some samples of our new blue LED chips, which were still under development at the time. They had taken those samples, packaged them, and then built a concept demo of a car dashboard made with LEDs. The idea was to show that with the addition of blue LEDs, you could make the dashboard any color you wanted. This was never intended to be a real product; it was just a technology demonstration. The Siemens team took the demo to Volkswagen (VW), where they showed it to some engineers. The engineers thought it was an interesting concept, but they didn't take it too seriously. Siemens left the demo with the VW team, not expecting much to come of it. Several weeks later, the CEO of VW, Ferdinand Piëch (the grandson of Ferdinand Porsche), happened to see the concept demo. When he scrolled through the different colors, he stopped on blue and said: "That's it. Blue should be the color of the dashboard in all of our cars." His team looked at him and said, "We don't think that's possible. Our supplier, Siemens, said this is just a prototype. Those blue LEDs aren't even in production yet." But Piëch was not deterred. He called his friend, the CEO of Siemens, and told him that blue dashboards were going to become a signature feature of all new models and he needed them to make it happen. He wanted them in the next year's models. This is what led to that urgent call from Norbert.

Norbert gave me the background and said we needed to figure out how to make the VW project a reality. I explained that these chips were still under development and not ready for production, let alone at the quality level and volume needed for an automotive customer. To complicate matters even more, they wanted an improved, lower-voltage version of the LED chip we had sampled—something else we hadn't figured out how to do yet. When I hung up the phone, I wasn't sure if I should jump for joy or jump out the window (don't worry, my office was on the first floor). I presented the opportunity to Neal Hunter, my boss (and the CEO), and John Edmond, our chief scientist for LEDs. We all knew this could be the first volume application ever for a blue LED. It had the potential to transform our company—to help us evolve from an R&D shop to a products company. The potential upside if we were successful was hard to imagine—but there seemed to be an equally significant downside if we weren't. The harsh reality was that we didn't have the capacity to deliver on the volume they were asking for, and we had no idea how to meet the voltage specification. We were going to have to build capacity and hope we could invent our way around the problem in time to support the launch of the new car models. The question became: Should we do this or not?

My initial instinct was to say no to the deal. I argued that it was just too risky. Given the legal agreements we would be forced to sign with a customer of this clout and size, the penalties for failing to deliver on our promises could easily bankrupt our company.

But Neal and John saw the risk from a completely different perspective. They knew we couldn't pass up a deal that could transform the company and put our products squarely on top of a burgeoning market (which it eventually did). They listened to my concerns, but then rightfully rebutted them by saying that we couldn't afford not to take the deal. By doing nothing, we were putting the company in even more jeopardy by possibly missing out on the biggest opportunity we could imagine at the time. They weren't afraid of failure and believed the risk was worth the opportunity it created and the potential return for our company. From their perspective, we were already betting on the success of these new chips; this deal was just accelerating our timeline. If we weren't able to ramp up our production capabilities for these products, we might go bankrupt anyway. When you frame risk that way, it clearly changes the equation—which was a valuable step along my journey to uncover my innovator's spirit.

THE REAL RISK IS DOING NOTHING

Have you ever stopped to wonder what innovation you appreciate most? The thing that makes the biggest impact on your daily life? Something that solves an important problem and adds real value? I asked this question one afternoon to my colleague Kate, who happens to be a working mom with three young children. She said she wanted to think about it overnight. While she was home that evening, she took a look around her house and the answer became obvious to her: the dishwasher. "We run one or two loads every day," she told me. "I remember in our old house, how many hours I spent standing at the kitchen sink washing dishes. The dishwasher changed my world." What's interesting is that Kate then decided to investigate who actually invented the dishwasher. And that's when she learned the story of Josephine Cochrane—who earned her first patent for an automated dishwasher in 1886.[1]

In 1870, Josephine and her husband, William, lived in Shelbyville, Illinois. William was a prominent merchant, investor, and rising politician. He enjoyed throwing dinner parties where he could show off his mansion and find reasons to break out a set of heirloom china that reportedly dated back to the 1600s. After one party, Josephine discovered that one of their servants had damaged one of the dishes while washing them. Furious, Cochrane insisted that she alone would clean those dishes from that day forward. It might have been a rash decision that she immediately regretted. But rather than reverse herself, she began to dream of a solution: an automated machine that would wash the dishes for her. She even sketched out a basic design: a rack that would hold the dishes in place as they were sprayed with warm soapy water heated by a copper boiler.

A few years later, in 1883, William Cochrane fell ill—and then suddenly passed away. Shocked by the loss of her husband, Josephine faced another harsh reality: Her husband hadn't been as well off as he led everyone to believe. In fact, he was deeply in debt—debt that Josephine was now forced to reckon with. What could she do?

She could build her dishwasher, she decided. As a woman at that time in history, that was no small decision to make. But Josephine decided she had nothing to lose. She was unafraid to fail.

So she took the design for her machine to some male engineers to see if they could help. It didn't go well. "I couldn't get men to do the things I wanted in my way until they had tried and failed on their own," she said. "And that was costly for me. They knew I knew nothing, academically, about mechanics, and they insisted on having their own way with my invention until they convinced themselves my way was the better way, no matter how I had arrived at it."[2]

Finally, she found a mechanic named George Butters who was willing to build a machine based on her design, a hand-powered model that served as the basis for her patent.

Now that she had her machine, Josephine needed customers. But her machine was still too large and expensive to sell to households. She needed to pitch to restaurants and big hotels like the Sherman House in Chicago instead—which she found more difficult than building her machine. She once told a reporter:

> The hardest part of getting into business . . . I think, [was] crossing the great lobby of the Sherman House alone. You cannot imagine what it was like in those days . . . for a woman to cross a hotel lobby alone. I had never been anywhere without my husband or father—the lobby seemed a mile wide. I thought I should faint at every step, but I didn't—and I got an $800 order as my reward.[3]

But Josephine didn't stop there in promoting her invention—which she initially contracted out to a factory to make for her. She not only was able to exhibit her machine during the 1893 World's Columbian Exposition in Chicago—where it earned distinction from judges who lauded it for "best mechanical construction, durability, and adaptation to its line of work"—but she convinced all of the restaurants at the fair to use her machine as well.[4] That additional exposure helped her open up a factory of her own, where she could ramp up production and introduce new models aimed at consumers. That company eventually became KitchenAid, which is now part of Whirlpool. More important, she changed people's lives with her innovation. All because she was willing to take a risk and do something no one else had.

I love Josephine Cochrane's story because it helps put the role of risk and failure in perspective when it comes to innovation. While it might at first seem obvious that pursuing innovation involves accepting some level of risk, there's something more subtle at work as well. Was Josephine's choice to try and turn her invention into a viable business risky? Sure. But wasn't there an even bigger risk? What was the risk if she did nothing? She could either try and possibly fail, or she could do nothing and guarantee failure. That's what great innovators inherently understand. And it's a critical part of uncovering your innovator's spirit. Yet this concept isn't easy for many of us to comprehend. How could doing nothing be riskier than gambling on an uncertain future?

It is easy to tell someone to be bold and take risks, especially when you have been doing it successfully for many years. But embracing risk can be extremely difficult for someone who has thrived on delivering predictable results and avoiding surprises at all costs. Consider a nugget of information that Clayton Christensen, the author of *The Innovator's Dilemma,* shared at an innovation and disruption symposium in 2017. He predicted that "50 percent of the four thousand colleges and universities in the U.S. will be bankrupt in ten to fifteen years."[5] If you were in the business of higher education, that should open your eyes. And yet, when this quote was presented in a meeting I attended with a group of university faculty, many of them tried to dismiss the quote as "fake news." I heard some quietly say, "I don't think he knows what he's talking about." Another person commented, "That can't be right, I'd like to see his analysis." Their reactions didn't surprise me. It's understandable that someone, especially a person who works in a slow-to-change environment like academia, might become defensive at the notion that their business model is about to be disrupted. It's been this way for a hundred years; why would things change now? Change is also likely to be seen by many as too risky. But how risky is it to just accept the status quo—to try and defend how things are? It's important to understand that people often avoid risk because they are afraid to fail. But what happens if you fail because you didn't take any risk? The point of this meeting was to get the group thinking about innovation in higher education. As we discussed this idea, I asked them to put aside their doubts for a little while and just assume that Christensen was right. If you believed this was going to happen, what would you do? When you embrace the premise, instead of arguing its merits, you create the opportunity to see the need for change.

EMBRACING THE NEED FOR RISK

Risk is a fundamental part of innovation, but many people seem to be confused with what it looks like in practice. I like to use the analogy of talking to a financial planner or investment advisor. Have you ever spoken with one? Or maybe you've completed an online investment questionnaire. If you have, you might remember that one of the first questions they usually ask is: How much risk are you willing to take? The second question they'll ask is: What kind of return do you want to make? That's when they pull out a chart that illustrates the relationship in a simple picture: The bigger return you want to make, the more risk you have to take. The math has been proven out time and again over many years of investing.

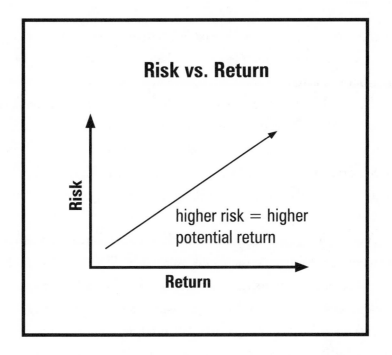

It turns out that this same risk-versus-return model applies to innovation. You may hear some business executives talk about the need to innovate while also managing risk, but that only leads to incremental ideas at best. You can't create real innovation unless you are willing to accept significant risk. It's math.

It's been my experience that everyone says they want to take risks—but their behaviors betray them as they do everything they can to manage or limit the amount of risk they are exposed to because they're trying to avoid failing. Let's face it, corporations reward predictability. CEOs and their management teams are measured on meeting their targets, more than on what they actually accomplish. I remember being advised to consider lowering our goals to ensure we hit them, instead of striving for an aggressive goal and possibly coming up short—even if the result would still exceed the lower goal. I understand that there is value in doing what you say you're going to do, but I believe there is far more value in what you actually do!

To develop something new that solves a significant problem and creates real value for the customer—my definition of innovation—you have to take risk proportional to the potential return. It's not a question of how much risk you should take. It starts with what you're trying to achieve and working backward to determine what risk is necessary to get there.

While this idea might seem simple and even obvious, it can be much harder for people to practice in real life. That's because of the management behaviors they've been taught. How many people do you know who were rewarded for taking a big risk—but who then failed? Probably not many. At work, in school, and at home, we've been taught to "be careful, it might not work out" instead of "take the risk, you'll win either way."

REFRAMING RISK

This brings us to the need to reframe risk. At Cree, we tried to reward people for taking risks even when they failed. Why? Because we always learned something when we took a big leap into the unknown. We were always better off when we pushed far ahead rather than tiptoeing in fear of failing. The one caveat was that everyone had to be willing to acknowledge when they made a bad decision, adjust immediately, and share what they learned with the team. If they did, we were learning; if they didn't, we were just creating new problems that had to be fixed later.

While we encouraged this kind of behavior among our people, it was hard for some to overcome their preexisting beliefs. I recall a conversation with Larry, one of my key leaders, who was also a military veteran and had worked for more than two decades at other large corporations before joining Cree to pursue innovation. In other words, he had a lot of management beliefs about failure and risk. He was a super smart and capable guy, but he struggled at times to embrace our belief that the real risk we faced was doing nothing. He said: "At my old company, I was trained to reduce or eliminate risk in order to deliver predictable outcomes. I was in the business of managing risk, not taking it. Here, you want me to take risk in order to deliver unpredictable outcomes with the goal to deliver more good results than bad. It's the exact opposite of everything I've been trained to do over the course of my career." The key for this leader was that he was self-aware enough to recognize where his personal gaps were and what he could do to try and overcome them in an effort to uncover his innovator's spirit.

No one likes to fail—especially innovators. You have to combine the risk-taking with an incredible passion and drive to succeed—a will to win. The goal isn't to fail; it's to take risk in order to accomplish something great—to innovate. Although you will have failures along the way, the key to innovation is to keep going, learning along the way, until you ultimately find a solution. This is what the psychologist Carol Dweck, a professor at Stanford University, calls having a "growth mindset."

In her book *Mindset: The New Psychology of Success*, Dweck describes an early experiment where she asked a group of children to solve a series of increasingly difficult puzzles. While she expected the kids to react differently to the challenges, she was surprised by the reaction of one ten-year-old boy when he was given a very difficult puzzle. "[He] pulled up his chair, rubbed his hands together, and smacked his lips, and cried out, 'I love a challenge!'" she writes.

Dweck saw similar reactions in other children as well, including one boy who, as he struggled with a puzzle, said, "You know, I was hoping this would be informative."[6]

Dweck writes that before the experiment, she assumed people either coped with failure or did not. What she didn't expect was that some people actually loved failure. "They knew that human qualities, such as intellectual skills, could be cultivated," she writes. "And that's what they were doing—getting smarter. Not only weren't they discouraged by failure, they didn't even think they were failing. They thought they were learning."[7]

It was this epiphany that led Dweck to coin her now well-known concept that people either embrace a fixed mindset, where a person's qualities are carved in stone, or a growth mindset, which she says is "based on the belief that your basic qualities are things you can cultivate through your efforts, your strategies, and help from others."[8] A growth mindset is an integral part of uncovering your innovator's spirit.

I listened to a 2015 interview between the comedian and podcaster Marc Maron and former president Barack Obama that took place during his second term in office, and I was struck by how President Obama was able to put his finger on exactly the point I'm trying to make here. When Maron asked President Obama what made him a better president, here's what he said:

> You lose fear. I was talking with somebody the other day about why I actually think I'm a better president and would be a better candidate if I were ever running again than I ever have been. And it's sort of like an athlete, you might slow down a little bit, you might not jump as high as you used to. But I know what I'm doing and

I'm fearless. You're not pretending to be fearless. When you get to that point, part of that fearlessness is because you've screwed up enough times. That you know that it's all happened. I've been through this, I've screwed up, I've been in the barrel tumbling down Niagara Falls, and I emerged and I lived. That is such a liberating feeling.[9]

When you look at risk and failure in this way, it doesn't seem all that risky anymore, does it? But it sure does drive innovation.

LEARNING FROM FAILURE

If I asked you to describe your biggest failure, what would you say? Who did you describe your failure to when it happened? What did you learn from the experience? What would you do differently the next time?

What I've learned is that some people are really uncomfortable talking about failure. Many times, people would answer my questions by saying something like "My biggest failure was that I worked too hard." That was never good enough for me, so I would keep prodding them to share a real failure with me. My goal was to see how they could take something negative—a failure—and turn it into a lesson that they learned—a positive. If they refused to share, or simply didn't have such an experience, I was pretty sure they wouldn't succeed at Cree. That's because I knew failure is the fuel of innovation.

Bill Gates, the cofounder of Microsoft and one of the world's richest men, also valued failure as a teacher. It might be hard to imagine Gates failing at anything. After all, Microsoft remains one of the world's most valuable companies even though Gates left it to run his foundation years ago. But Microsoft's success as a software innovator didn't occur in a straight line. In fact, in his book *Business @ the Speed of Thought*, Gates shares many of the failed initiatives they tried over the years—efforts he called "worthy failures":

> To win big, sometimes you have to take big risks. Big bets mean big failures as well as successes. Today, with the benefit of hindsight, it's easy to believe that Microsoft's current success was preordained. Yet at the time we made our big bets—including the founding of the company as the first microcomputer software firm—most people scoffed. Many industry leaders hesitated to move to new technologies. They learned a hard lesson. If you decline to take risks early, you'll decline in the market later. If you bet big, though, only a few of these risks have to succeed to provide for your future.[10]

Gates also talks about how Microsoft learned even when it failed. He writes: "Once you embrace unpleasant news not as negative but as evidence of a need for change, you aren't defeated by it. You're learning from it. It's all in how you approach failures. And believe me, we know a lot about failures at Microsoft." He then shares examples about how their early spreadsheet program couldn't make headway against a competing product, Lotus 1-2-3. They also spent half a decade building a database product called Omega that they eventually abandoned. They failed at launching their own personal digital assistant to compete against the Apple Newton. Apparently, the company also tried launching a series of internet shows on its Microsoft Network—which flopped. Then there were the hundreds of millions of dollars, and countless developer hours, they invested in a partnership with IBM to build a new operating system called OS/2. But when IBM canceled the project, it was all for nothing. Or was it?

"The weight of all of our failures could make me too depressed to come into work," Gates writes. "Instead I am excited about the challenges and by how we can use today's bad news to help solve tomorrow's problems."[11]

Rather than take those failures as defeats, Gates and his team turned them into learning opportunities. In other words, failure became the fuel for innovation. From the failed early spreadsheet efforts, for instance, Microsoft Excel emerged to become the standard spreadsheet of a generation. The lessons from the Omega failure helped them create Microsoft Access—which set a new standard for desktop databases. The abandoned internet shows evolved into more practical information, like Microsoft Expedia and Investor, and the lessons learned from the OS/2 debacle helped them create Windows NT—which became the standard operating system for many if not most PC users at the time. "Learning from mistakes and constantly improving products is a key in all successful companies," Gates writes.[12]

DON'T LET FEAR LEAD TO REGRET

Chances are that you've bought something at some time in your life on Amazon.com. You may even have bought this book there! But even if you're reading this at your local library, you likely know that Amazon's founder, Jeff Bezos, is one of the most successful entrepreneurs of all time. Of course, Amazon now sells far more than just books. Not only is it an online retailer of seemingly everything, but it's also a logistics company, and its computer servers host an increasing number of the world's websites. There's even a phrase, "the Amazon Effect," that's used to describe what happens to an industry when Amazon moves in to disrupt it.[13] In short, Amazon has changed how we live our lives. But it almost didn't happen. What if Jeff Bezos—who had a good job, as well as a new wife— thought that starting his fledgling bookstore was too risky, that he would fail?

When Bezos told his boss that he was going to leave his Wall Street firm to start an online bookstore, they took a walk around Central Park. His boss told Bezos he understood his entrepreneurial impulse, but he reminded him that he had a great job with the firm. The boss also told Bezos that the firm might eventually compete with his new venture. Given all that, why take the risk? Bezos agreed to give his boss's advice some thought.

Bezos's wife, MacKenzie, was supportive of his idea to go out on his own. But he still wasn't sure what to do. That's when he came up with what he called a regret-minimization framework to help him make his decision either way. His goal, Bezos later said, was to put his decision in perspective: Would he later regret not acting? As Brad Stone quotes Bezos in *The Everything Store*:

> I knew when I was eighty that I would never, for example, think about why I walked away from my 1994 Wall Street bonus right in the middle of the year at the worst possible time. That kind of thing just isn't something you worry about when you're eighty years old. At the same time, I knew that I might sincerely regret not having participated in this thing called the Internet that I thought was going to be a revolutionizing event. When I thought about it that way . . . it was incredibly easy to make the decision.[14]

Bezos reportedly embraced that same mantra as he was building Amazon into the dominant company it is today. He put the notion of risk and failure into context with his philosophy that "nine times out of ten, you're going to fail. But every once in a while, you'll hit a home run that in business terms is more like one thousand runs. Given a ten percent chance of a one hundred times payoff, you should take that bet every time."[15] To say that another way, he'd rather fail nine times out of ten if he has the chance to create a truly innovative product as a result. And if he didn't at least swing for the home run, he might always wonder how things might have ended up differently. When you're willing to embrace risk—and be unafraid of failure—you also minimize the chances that you'll regret your actions later on.

Bezos even made a similar point to Amazon's investors in a shareholders' letter when he wrote: "To invent you have to experiment, and if you know in advance that it's going to work, it's not an experiment. Most large organizations embrace the idea of invention, but are not willing to suffer the string of failed experiments necessary to get there."[16] So when we think of Amazon as a dominant player in our lives, we might forget about its failed ventures such as its travel booking site, Amazon Destinations, or its eBay competitor, Amazon Auctions—both of which were shelved. Then there's Amazon's first foray into the smartphone market, the Fire Phone, which was canceled with some $170 million in unsold phones sitting in warehouses. "I've made billions of dollars of failures at Amazon.com," Bezos once said. "None of those things are fun, but they don't matter. What really matters is that companies that don't continue to experiment—companies that don't embrace failure—they eventually get in a desperate position, where the only thing they can do is make a 'Hail Mary' bet at the very end."[17]

His point is that betting everything on the last play of the game—a do-or-die, winner-take-all bet—is exactly the wrong kind of risk to take. By then it's too late. "If you decide that you're going to do only the things you know are going to work, you're going to leave a lot of opportunity on the table," Bezos once said.[18] That's why Bezos, in that same shareholder letter, described his company this way: "One area where I think we are especially distinctive is failure. I believe we are the best place in the world to fail (we have plenty of practice!)."[19]

Can you imagine your organization adopting a mindset like this? Or, better yet, a best practice based on these beliefs? The paradox is that if you want to unleash your innovator's spirit, you actually need to throw typical best practices out the window and go beyond them.

CHAPTER NINE RECAP

Belief: The real risk is in doing nothing.

Behavior: Be unafraid of failure.

KEY INSIGHTS

Embrace risk. To develop something new that solves a significant problem and creates real value, you have to take risk proportional to the desired return.

Failure is the fuel of innovation. You will encounter failure. But failure is an opportunity to learn. The key to innovation is to keep going, learning from each failure along the way, until you ultimately find a solution.

The real risk is in doing nothing. You can try and possibly fail, or you can do nothing and guarantee failure.

CHAPTER TEN

Go Beyond Best Practice

"The person who follows the crowd will usually go no further than the crowd. The person who walks alone is likely to find himself in places no one has ever seen before."
—Albert Einstein[1]

IN MY EXPERIENCE, YOU RARELY achieve something remarkable that you were not trying to achieve in the first place. Without the mindset to try and do something great, you're only likely to achieve average. And to find your innovator's spirit, you need to embrace the notion that whatever you do today can be done better tomorrow. There is no endpoint, just the next point. That's how you keep pushing yourself to go beyond the status quo. And if you know there is always a better idea, it keeps you from getting stuck in a box.

So how do you uncover something new if you simply follow the blueprint laid down by someone else? You can't. That's why "best practices" don't work for innovation. They only lead to the same results that others have already realized, not something new. They're a way to settle for good enough and avoid risk. If you want to lead innovation, you need to keep searching for a better way—to go beyond the best practice—as you indulge your curiosity on the journey to explore the unknown.

EXPLORING THE INVISIBLE

What happens when you follow the rules, come across a great discovery, and are then ignored? How well do best practices guide you when you're trying to discover something no one even believes is possible? What obstacles are you willing to overcome to turn a discovery into an innovation that actually solves a real problem? To some degree, this was the path taken by the brilliant scientist Marie Curie, where she was forced to overcome the scientific establishment to bring her innovations to life. Originally born in Warsaw, Poland, in 1867 with the name Marya Sklodowska, Curie—who took the last name of her husband and fellow scientist Pierre—broke molds and glass ceilings on her way to paving an entire field of science we now call radiology.[2]

As a woman, Curie faced constant sexism in her work in which male scientists either overlooked her achievements or credited her husband for her work. Another challenge Curie and her husband faced was a lack of adequate resources or funding. That meant while their peers worked in modern laboratories, the Curies were forced to run their experiments inside a decrepit warehouse that had once housed dead bodies. Nothing was easy. But through sheer determination and persistence, the Curies built on the work from other scientists like Henri Becquerel to eventually uncover two new radioactive elements: polonium (named for her native Poland) and radium.

What made the discovery so notable was that most scientists at the time thought that the atom was the smallest bit of matter possible. Her theory was that radioactivity was caused by atoms falling apart. If that was the case, then atoms must be made up of even smaller parts. Her work also overturned the belief and prevailing best practice that one element cannot turn into another. As she wrote in her diary: "There can be no doubt of the existence of these new elements, but to make chemists admit their existence, it was necessary to isolate them."[3] By ignoring that best practice, and by using the clues given by radioactivity, Curie was able to break new ground. One of Curie's biographers puts it this way: "Her greatest achievement was employing an entirely new method to discover elements by measuring their radioactivity. In the next decade scientists who located the source and composition of radioactivity made more discoveries concerning the atom and its structure than in all the centuries that had gone before."[4] In other words, she gave scientists a whole new way to look at the world.

Marie and Pierre, along with Becquerel, shared a Nobel Prize in Physics in 1903 for their work—making Curie the first woman to ever win the award. Curie said at the time: "Our research on new radioactive substances gave birth to a scientific movement."[5]

After her husband's tragic accidental death in 1906, Curie continued her work as well as her impact on the world. In 1911, she received her second Nobel Prize, this time in Chemistry, for her further work in radioactivity, what she called "the chemistry of the invisible"—making her the first and only person to ever win separate Nobel Prizes in those disciplines. Curie is noted as saying: "A great discovery does not issue from a scientist's head ready-made, like Minerva springing fully armed from Jupiter's head; it is the fruit of an accumulation of preliminary work."[6]

At this point in her life Curie evolved from a world-class inventor into an innovator, as she used her discoveries to solve a real problem and create immeasurable value by saving lives. Despite widespread skepticism, Curie developed small, mobile X-ray units in 1914 that could be mounted in cars and deployed to the World War I battlefields in Europe. Curie and her seventeen-year-old daughter, Irène, took these mobile X-ray units, dubbed "Les Petites Curies," to the frontlines to perform X-rays on the wounded, which helped better diagnose various fractures and bullet wounds. The machines, which diagnosed more than one million wounded soldiers during the course of the war, were described as "the perfect marriage of technology and practicality."[7] Similar devices, called fluoroscopy machines, are still used today in modern hospitals.

After the war, Curie turned her efforts into the field of cancer research by creating the Radium Institute (now called the Curie Institute), where she helped show how radioactive elements could be used to treat cancer. Ironically, what Curie never fully realized was how her work constantly exposed her and her research team to harmful radiation—something that would eventually lead to Curie's death in 1934. Reportedly, the clothes she wore at the time, now preserved, remain radioactive (her daughter would also die as a result of accumulated radiation).

No doubt, our world is better today because of Marie Curie's drive to go beyond the accepted best practices and to discover something entirely new—and then find a way to turn that discovery into a solution to humankind's problems.

CREATING BETTER PRACTICES

The first step in the pursuit of the impossible is to ignore the past—which can be extremely difficult because best practices are prevalent in every industry. Semiconductors are no exception. The blue LED might never have been invented if someone hadn't come along who was willing to break the established rules.

The major LED companies had been making red and green LEDs for decades. As they investigated how to create blue LEDs, they realized they needed a different material system to create blue light. As they worked on the basic science, they discovered there were too many defects in the materials to make an LED—or so they thought. These companies were experts at making LEDs and had invented the best practices. The problem with experts is that they know what's not possible. What they don't know, however, is how to achieve the impossible. In the case of trying to invent blue LEDs, their assumptions about defects were based on how red and green LEDs worked. When they applied those same principles to this new material system, it was clear to them that it would never work. So they gave up.

Which created an opportunity for Cree and Nichia, a Japanese chemical company, as neither of us was in the red and green LED business. We didn't have the same boundary conditions. We weren't limited by what worked for red and green LEDs. We weren't limited by best practices. Instead, we believed it must be possible and looked for a better way. We tried things that shouldn't have worked. And in the end, what we learned is that blue LEDs operate in ways no one expected. Those defects that stopped the other companies were actually not a problem for blue LEDs, and our companies ended up changing the industry and disrupting the balance of power in the LED business.

If you want to think about someone who was willing to challenge conventional thinking, consider the story of Galileo Galilei. He was an Italian scientist during the late 1500s and early 1600s, a time when many believed that the earth was the center of the universe—and that the sun revolved around the earth. The all-powerful Catholic Church reinforced that "fact." But Galileo wasn't content with that story. He knew there must be a better explanation. The church's story didn't match up with his observations of the stars and planets like Venus, Jupiter, and Saturn in the night sky. He reportedly said, "All truths are easy to understand once they are discovered; the point is to discover them."[8] And to do that, sometimes you have to have the courage to look past what others tell you is the truth. Unfortunately for Galileo, the pope at the time, Urban VIII, found his views heretical—even though the scientist made his arguments through mathematical facts—and forced Galileo to spend the rest of his life under house arrest.[9] Fortunately for the rest of us, Galileo continued to expand on his breakthrough work in the field of physics and his improved version of the telescope—which became the kind of innovation that eventually changed how we saw the universe around us. Galileo inspired pioneers that followed him like Albert Einstein and Stephen Hawking to look beyond best practice in search of better ideas. And it is why he is now known as one of the fathers of modern science.

We're under constant pressure to embrace best practices and conventional thinking. They are the basis of good management and they work. There is no risk in following a best practice, except that it won't lead to something new. Innovation is about discovering a better practice, and once you do, finding something even better.

DON'T LEAVE WELL ENOUGH ALONE

If someone gave you the money to start your own retail business, would you model yourself after another company? If so, who would it be and why? Or would you try to do something completely different—to come up with an entirely new business model? That's basically what Sam Walton did when he created Walmart, one of the most successful retailers (and companies) of all time.

It's just about impossible to visit any town across the country that doesn't have a Walmart or Sam's Club. The company, which opened its first store in 1962,[10] now has more than 5,300 locations in the United States. But one of the keys to that spectacular growth was the belief of founder Sam Walton that he needed to do things differently than everyone else, as he wrote in his autobiography:

> Swim upstream. Go the other way. Ignore the conventional wisdom. If everybody else is doing it one way, there's a good chance you can find your niche by going in exactly the opposite direction. But be prepared for a lot of folks to wave you down and tell you you're headed the wrong way.[11]

Walton got his start in the retail business in 1945 when he and his wife borrowed money from her parents and bought a Ben Franklin variety store in Newport, Arkansas. It seemed like a risky move since he had no experience in running a retail shop. But as he wrote: "It was a real blessing for me to be so green and ignorant, because it was from that experience that I learned a lesson which has stuck with me all through the years: you can learn from any-body."[12] That included watching how his main competitor across the street ran his business. In other words, Walton wasn't counting on running his store the way everyone else was; he wanted to run it the way it needed to be run.

What's interesting is that Walton was a Ben Franklin franchisee and he had been sent to a school where all franchisees were taught how to run their stores—from operations to accounting—literally by their book. But, as he wrote: "It didn't take me long to start experimenting—that's just the way I am and always have been. Pretty soon I was laying on promotional programs of my own, and then I started buying merchandise directly from manufacturers."[13] Walton was always looking for new suppliers who could offer his customers more variety. He was searching for better.

That, Walton wrote, was the start of the philosophies that he later carried over when he started his first Walmart. He realized early on that by cutting the best deals with suppliers directly, he could sell his products at a lower price. And even though his margins were lower, he made more money by selling in volume.

The problem was that as a franchisee, he was forced to buy most of his goods through the franchise—which severely limited the growth of his business. That said, he couldn't help himself from pushing those boundaries. "I could never leave well enough alone, and in fact, I think my constant fiddling and meddling with the status quo may have been one of my biggest contributions to the later success of Wal-Mart," he wrote.[14]

Due to an oversight he made in signing his franchise contract and lease, Walton was forced to sell his store—which had become the most successful in his region—to his landlord when he wouldn't renew the lease. It was a low point in his life. But he was ready to keep fighting. David Glass, who served as Walmart's CEO from 1988 to 2000, said: "Two things about Sam Walton distinguish him from everyone else I know. First, he gets up every day bound and determined to improve something. Second, he is less afraid of being wrong than anyone I've ever known. And once he sees he's wrong, he just shakes it off and heads in another direction."[15]

Heading in another direction led Walton to Bentonville, Arkansas (which would become Walmart's headquarters), where he and his wife bought another Ben Franklin franchise, only they called it Walton's 5&10. A few years later, Walton bought a building in Fayetteville and opened another Walton's 5&10. He eventually began to open stores all over the state. At the same time, he also saw that the retail industry was about to be disrupted by national discount chains. Rather than wait for them to come, he decided to become one instead. But everyone he approached about partnering with him wasn't interested. They didn't think discounting would work as a national business. So Walton and his family did it themselves by opening the first Walmart in Rogers, Arkansas, betting everything they had in doing so. He wrote in his autobiography:

> We were innovating, experimenting, and expanding. Somehow over the years, folks have gotten the impression that Wal-Mart was something I dreamed up out of the blue as a middle-aged man, and that it was just this great idea that turned into an overnight success. It's true I was forty-four when we opened our first Wal-Mart in 1962, but the store was totally an outgrowth of everything we'd been doing since Newport—another case of me being unable to leave well enough alone, another

experiment. And like most other overnight successes, it was about twenty years in the making.[16]

It wasn't long before Walton was breaking all of the rules most other retailers followed. One example was that most variety stores at the time stuck to selling in just a single state. Walton thought nothing of doing business in four or more states, all in a single day.

Through his experiments with his growing number of stores, Walton also learned how he could expand his business by building larger stores—again bucking what was accepted practice among his competitors. "We paid absolutely no attention whatsoever to the way things were supposed to be done, you know, the way the rules of retail said it had to be done," Walton wrote.[17]

Walton would continue to innovate and swim upstream from the rest of the retail industry by creating one of the world's most efficient logistics networks. The company could source its materials from all over the world and sell them for the lowest price possible. By doing that, Walton completely changed the retail industry in the United States—and the way most Americans went shopping.

Walton, who passed away in 1992, is considered the greatest retailer of his time. But in my opinion, he was an even better innovator. He defined a whole new way of thinking about retail, which became industry best practices. After he left, the company continued to grow and refine his ideas, but they didn't continue to innovate. Today, Walmart is facing incredible challenges in its business from e-commerce players like Amazon, who created a new business model using technology to make the shopping experience even better. I have a sense that if Sam Walton were still around, his inability to leave well enough alone would have helped him respond to this challenge both sooner and with new and better ideas.

MAKING THE IMPOSSIBLE POSSIBLE

You might recall the story I told in Chapter Nine about how we landed the Volkswagen (VW) LED design win, despite my worries that it was too much of a risk to take. I also mentioned it turned out to be a landmark moment in Cree's history—one that put our company's growth on a new trajectory. But the story didn't end with us deciding to take the risk; it was just beginning. The truth is, we didn't have any idea how we were going to ramp up our LED capacity so we could meet VW's requirements.

The first problem we had to solve was figuring out how to meet the voltage specification. Only five percent of our LEDs actually met the spec, which was far too low a number to make the math work. We needed to find a way to get the yield much, much higher to have any chance to meet the demand. Our customer, Siemens (who bought our chips and then sold the LEDs to VW), insisted that it send a team to our factory to help us out. We didn't have any idea how to solve this problem, so it seemed like a good idea. Siemens ended up sending four senior engineers to work with us for several months. While they didn't know much about our specific blue LED technology, they were experts at LED manufacturing and operations. Their job was to help us figure out how to reduce the voltage and increase the yield by at least ten times.

The Siemens guys looked at the problem and concluded that we would need to find a series of continuous improvements to achieve our goal. They said it would take many small steps to reduce the voltage. These guys were the experts with years of combined experience, so I figured that was our best course of action. They seemed to know everything about the industry best practices. John and Gerry, the two Cree scientists driving the program, didn't agree with me or with the Siemens guys. They said we could never get the breakthrough we needed through continuous improvements. They said we needed to focus on finding the one big lever, the big idea that would solve the entire equation.

Finding myself in the middle of these two very different approaches, I told John and Gerry that we would run a parallel process where they could try their experiments while the Siemens team focused on continuous improvements. The Cree team had no problem with this approach; they were focused on finding a break-through. On the other hand, the Siemens team was frustrated and complained that the Cree guys weren't listening to them—they were ignoring their years of experience. And they did. John and Gerry attended the meetings on continuous improvement, but then just went back to looking for a better idea.

Then, while working one weekend, Dave, a Cree engineer, ran an experiment looking for a big lever where he put an LED wafer into one of the production tools and he got an unexpected result: The voltage on most of the LED chips was now much lower. He was surprised because that shouldn't have happened in this process step. After looking through the results, he realized that the machine he had used had been set up with the recipe for a different product. He had stumbled upon the breakthrough we needed. We now had a way of making lower-voltage chips—all because our team didn't believe in conforming to best practice. What we learned in the pro-cess is that there is rarely a path to innovation through continuous improvement, because the big breakthroughs usually come from discontinuous ideas.

After we overcame the voltage issue, the Siemens team went home and we were on our way to ramping up the factory when I received another call from Norbert Hiller, who was running the LED business at Siemens. He wanted to let me know that VW couldn't buy our chips unless our factory passed a quality audit. Our quality system needed to meet their automotive standards. I knew that was going to be a big problem, because we didn't actually have a quality system for them to audit. I asked Norbert how long we had until the VW guys showed up, and he said they would be in North Carolina in a few weeks. "OK," I said, "we'll figure something out." I hung up and made a series of calls. I finally made contact with a consultant who specialized in setting up quality systems for automotive suppliers. I explained what our problem was and asked him for help. He told me that he would send me some things to start working on right away and then come visit us the following week.

After we gave the consultant a tour of the factory, we talked strategy. He told us there was no way we were going to have a quality system in place by the time of the visit. We determined that we could prepare a plan and outline of what the system was going to look like, but it would take at least six months to do all the work. We only had a week to work with, so we decided that whenever the VW auditor asked to see our quality system, I would honestly say we didn't have one yet, but we were working to put one in place. I admit this was not a great plan. I had worked in the automotive industry earlier in my career, and it seemed like there was no way this could work. How do they audit a quality system that doesn't exist yet? I was worried that we might have come all this way for nothing. As I took the VW auditors through the plant and they asked questions, I focused on talking about our process to make the LED chips. And every time they asked about the quality system, I said we were working on it but didn't have one yet. I must have given that answer more than twenty times over their two-day visit. I was pretty sure we were about to score a zero on the audit.

As a final stop in the process tour, I showed the auditors our testing area and explained how our proprietary tester worked. I showed them how we tested the LED chips and pointed out that we knew the technology was immature, so we had invested a lot of time and money into our testing methodology. When a chip passed our test, we had a very high confidence that the long-term reliability of that LED would be good. I thought my explanation sounded pretty good but figured it was too little, too late.

As we met with the auditors later that day to review the results, I prepared myself to hear bad news. And as the lead auditor began to speak in his accented English, he seemed to confirm my fears when he said, "You have none of the things we would expect to find in the quality system of an automotive supplier." He then added, "However, based on the testing methodology you have and your commitment to build a quality system, we will conditionally pass you as a supplier to VW." I just about fell out of my chair. I almost blurted out, "Are you sure?" We broke every rule possible that you needed to follow to get a product designed into a car—and yet we had somehow been approved. We didn't have a best practice quality system, but our testing methodology was a better practice. It truly seemed like we had made it at that point.

Wrong.

A few weeks after we passed the audit, I got another call from my buddy Norbert at Siemens. (We spent so much time working together on the VW project that he eventually joined the Cree team to run our LED business.) We now were just a few months away from shipping our LEDs to VW. But Norbert had some more bad news. He said VW was adding a new specification to the contract: Our LEDs now had to pass a new test, something called a Class 2 electrostatic discharge (ESD) test. Basically, it meant that the LEDs had to survive being shocked by high voltage. I was stunned.

I told Norbert that I didn't think anyone tested LEDs that way and I was pretty sure that blue LEDs were very sensitive to static discharge. This was a crazy request. He was sympathetic but firm: VW was insisting that our LEDs couldn't be designed into the cars unless they could pass that test.

We were stuck yet again. If we didn't figure this out, we could be looking at the end before we even got started. And we had no idea where to start. ESD was not a problem we had tried to solve before. There was no time to redesign the LED to make it pass. Even if there was, we had no idea what caused our chips to be sensitive to ESD. I remember spending a weekend with John, Gerry, and Doug, a software guru who had developed our testers. We started by testing some of our chips according to the Class 2 ESD test standard and found that some passed and some failed—but we had to guarantee that all of the chips we sent to VW would pass. It didn't look good. Our best idea was to somehow use our testing methodology to weed out the bad ones. But all of the literature we read told us that even if an LED survived such a test, it would be damaged and less reliable as a result. They would fail sooner than if they hadn't been tested. In other words, every LED we tested this way would be worthless.

But John said, "Let's try it anyway, because otherwise we're screwed." So John, Gerry, and Doug spent the weekend trying different tests to stress the diodes, while I hovered in the background hoping for a miracle. We wanted to find a way to identify the weak ones without harming the good ones. Eventually, they came up with a type of reverse-bias test that didn't seem logical, and when we performed it, half the diodes died and half lived. But the good news was that the ones that lived weren't weaker as a result. They continued to pass the Class 2 ESD test. The bad news was that our yield would be cut to just fifty percent. So I went back to Norbert at Siemens and told him that we had found a way to pass their test—but they would have to pay twice as much per LED in the beginning until we could find a way to improve the yields. Fortunately for us, they agreed to that deal, which began Cree's transformation into a real product company. And we learned again that innovation is often counter to what the experts believe will work—which is why it has never been done before.

BREAKING THE MOLD

When you think of a company that has continually flown in the face of industry best practices, you don't have to look further than Southwest Airlines. In a sector where so many airlines struggle to make money, or even stay in business over the long run (think about a few bygone names like Eastern, Pan Am, and TWA), Southwest has posted a remarkable run of profits for forty-six straight years.[18] But the reason why Southwest's performance bucks the trends of its competitors is because it rejected the industry best practices right from the start.

Reportedly hatched on a bar napkin by San Antonio entrepreneurs Rollin King, John Parker, and Herb Kelleher, Southwest Airlines was incorporated in 1967. But that was just the first volley in a series of legal battles where established airlines in the market like Braniff fought to keep Southwest from ever getting off the ground. It took four years of legal fighting, until June 18, 1971, before Southwest was ready to change the game for how an airline could be run profitably while also offering the lowest prices. The book *Nuts!: Southwest Airlines' Crazy Recipe for Business and Personal Success*, which captures the company's start-up story, frames it this way: "From day one, Southwest challenged the assumption that permanently reduced fares would cut revenue."[19]

The founders understood that if they wanted to create a low-cost airline, they needed to do just about everything differently from what their competitors were doing. Said Kelleher, who would become the airline's iconic CEO: "We've never tried to be like other airlines. From the very beginning we told our people, 'Question it. Challenge it.' Remember, decades of conventional wisdom have sometimes led the airline industry into huge losses."[20]

Doing things differently meant serving peanuts instead of full meals,[21] or coming up with a new way to assign seating on a first-come basis. There was also the time Southwest fought back in a fare war against a far bigger rival by offering a bottle of alcohol—a choice of whiskey, scotch, or vodka—as a bonus for buying a ticket, a practice that made the airline the largest liquor distributor in Texas for a while.[22] Can you imagine anyone else adopting that as a best practice?

Another of the key priorities Southwest adopted early on was to make sure its planes were flying as often as possible. That meant making quick turns on the ground—ten to fifteen minutes—before a plane would take off again. That led the airline to operate out of less busy airports where the planes wouldn't get bogged down in queues. Think Chicago's Midway instead of O'Hare, or Dallas's Love Field instead of Dallas/Fort Worth International. Similarly going against the industry grain, Southwest prioritized flying short point-to-point trips as opposed to adopting the hub-and-spoke model most of the other major airlines used. Kelleher thought that the hub model, which was designed to gain more market share, was a losing proposition. The only reason Southwest would enter a market was if it could make money.

That same mantra exists today as Southwest continues to turn the tables on the accepted wisdom of the airline crowd. For many years, I wouldn't fly Southwest. I wanted my assigned seat and was willing to pay a little more. But then I tried it. The flight attendants were having fun and it rubbed off on me. We left on time and arrived on time. The price was low. And I could check my bag for free. It wasn't the cost that mattered to me; it was how much more pleasant the rest of the process was. They had eliminated the chaos created when everyone carries on their bags. By breaking the mold, they had built something better.

THE DRIVE NEVER ENDS

The innovator's spirit is about pursuing something better. I remember in the early days of Cree, we used to say that as soon as we hit $100 million in revenue, we would have accomplished everything we set out to do. We could then relax and hit the golf course. But $100 million came and went. Then so did $500 million and $1 billion—and we kept going. We realized there was always something more, something better to strive for. It was much more exciting to discover what comes next rather than being satisfied with what we had already accomplished. It was the journey that motivated us, not the milestones or destinations along the way.

As you pursue something better, you should expect to face resistance along the way. This was an ongoing challenge at Cree, either from people within the company who had become satisfied with our success or from outsiders like our board of directors. Despite our success, our board would often ask us why we weren't more committed to following industry best practices. If you think about their role, this isn't really a surprise. A public company like Cree needs to prioritize its returns to the shareholders. And for our board members, it made sense that we should embrace best practices to deliver on that obligation. While I understood their perspective, the suggestion made me crazy. We were focused on innovation—that's what really created value for our shareholders. Best practice only leads to average. Didn't they see that we would best serve our shareholders if we instead pursued better ideas? So I spent a lot of time helping them see the logic of our approach. I'm sure some of the board members were never fully comfortable with our disregard for best practices, but I appreciate that they gave us the freedom to do what we thought was best for the business.

If you want your innovator's spirit to thrive, be prepared to continually convince others that there is always a better way. And remember that you will never achieve perfection.

CHAPTER TEN RECAP

Belief: Whatever we do today can be done better tomorrow.

Behavior: Go beyond best practice.

KEY INSIGHTS

Pursue something better. Don't leave well enough alone. There is no endpoint, just the next point. You rarely achieve something remarkable that you were not trying to achieve in the first place.

Best practices don't work. They only lead to the same results that others have already realized—not something new.

The problem with experts is that they know what's not possible. What they don't know, however, is how to achieve the impossible.

CHAPTER ELEVEN

Don't Wait
for Perfection

*"Just start. Don't wait for perfection. Just start
and let the work teach you."*

—Jacqueline Novogratz

IF YOU HAVE THE CHOICE of making two decisions in a month
and getting them both right, or making ten decisions and getting
seven wrong, which is better? Whenever I've asked this question to
people in interviews, they generally choose the first option. After
all, going two-for-two has a nice ring to it. That's a zero percent
failure rate—isn't that the definition of perfection? Maybe for some
people. But when you're trying to innovate, the better option is to

be wrong seven times out of ten. Why? Because you were right three times—a fifty percent better result. More important, every "wrong" decision was an opportunity to learn and make a more informed decision the next time. That's how you fuel innovation.

You may be thinking this sounds similar to the concept of "failing fast," which gets plenty of attention in the press. But there is an important distinction. The objective is not to fail, but to make decisions and understand there will be mistakes in pursuit of the knowledge that will ultimately drive success. I've seen this concept misapplied by people on numerous occasions. And whenever I challenged it, I was told that they thought the goal was to fail fast. This concept is not an excuse for failure. It is understanding that it's better to make a decision with what you know and learn from it as opposed to waiting to act. The result is that you wind up net ahead. To do that, you need to get comfortable with imperfection and change. You need to recognize that there can often be more value in moving fast, learning, and improving along the way—rather than waiting to act until you get something "just right." It is learning that ultimately drives innovation, so you want to maximize it.

As you pursue your innovator's spirit, one of the challenges you will face is that you will often have no idea of how to get to your goal. It takes a certain mindset to embark on a journey without a plan to get to your destination. So how do you develop the mindset to deal with this inherent uncertainty? It may not sound too complicated on the surface, but I find that most people are actually quite uncomfortable with this idea. They've been taught they should have a clear plan and a specific definition of what the final outcome looks like, including a timeline and milestones. When they try to apply this structured approach to solving a new problem, they realize there are too many unknowns. So they stop and spend even more time trying to resolve those open items—typically through more research on the subject, looking for clues from other experts or in the literature. They forget they're trying to do something new, something that has never been done before. By definition, the answers to their questions are not known. Eventually, they get stuck. This is what I call waiting for perfection.

THE POWER OF DIRECTIONALLY CORRECT

What do you do when you realize that "you don't know what you don't know"? Think about it for a few minutes. What do you do? What I saw work time and again is to stop trying to know everything and start doing something. You don't need to know exactly how it's going to work out, you only need to be directionally correct.

How do you implement this idea of being directionally correct?

1. Pick a direction.

2. Take your best idea.

3. Try it and see what happens.

4. Use what you learned to adjust and try again.

In other words, you run some experiments. No matter what the result is, after each experiment you have more information. This information can be used to inform the next step and the direction becomes a little clearer. And this concept doesn't just apply to product or technical innovation. A designer named Meg Busse framed this idea in a piece for the *Stanford Social Innovation Review*:

> Experimentation may seem unpredictable or risky given the serious issues that social organizations are tackling, but the world is changing faster than we can create impact

using known methods. By experimenting to source new ideas, organizations can take advantage of multiple opportunities for learning, including crowdsourcing information, testing a process or tool, and empowering the community to contribute to the solution. . . . The more often organizations experiment, the faster they gain data to inform the next potential breakthrough.[1]

When you start to pursue a new problem, you can't possibly know how it's going to turn out. And you don't need to know—just start heading in a direction. It will quickly become clear if it is the right direction or not, then you adjust and keep moving.

The point is that if you want to achieve something no one has ever done before—or to do something better than anyone who came before you—you can't wait for it to come to you. You have to start taking action to make it happen.

CHASING EXCELLENCE

As a lifelong fan of the Chicago Bears football team, I have spent much of my life believing there was nothing good about the Green Bay Packers. This is one of the oldest rivalries in pro football, and growing up near Chicago, my loyalty was clearly to the Bears. So you can imagine my surprise when I joined the board of trustees at Marquette University and learned that John, the board chair, was also on the board of the Green Bay Packers. Marquette is located in Milwaukee, Wisconsin, so it's expected that I would be surrounded by Packers fans. But this was the first person I ever met who actually served on the football team's board. Prior to meeting John, I didn't realize the Packers even had a board of directors.

At the end of my first year on the Marquette board, John presented each trustee with a small Christmas gift to thank us for our service to the university. The gift was a brass sticky-note holder with a quote engraved on it that read: "We are going to relentlessly chase perfection . . . I am not remotely interested in being just good." He told us that the quote was from a speech given by Vince Lombardi, the legendary Packers coach. I didn't want to like the quote; it was from the leader of the hated Packers. But I managed to look past the sports rivalry and realize that he had captured something that was far more important. He had captured an element of the innovator's spirit. He had defined the mindset required to do something that has never been done before—to do something innovative.

This quote became a fixture on my desk, and it made me want to learn more about Vince Lombardi. Under Lombardi's leadership, the Packers won five league championships and the first two Super Bowls, in 1967 and 1968. What made the success of Lombardi's teams more remarkable is that the Packers were the worst team in the league when he arrived as coach in 1959. During the Lombardi era, the team never had a losing record; his winning percentage as a coach remains one of the best of all time. And the key reason behind the turnaround was that Lombardi didn't believe in just following what other teams did; he wanted to find a better way to play the game.

Lombardi grew up in Brooklyn, New York, and later attended Fordham University, where he starred as an offensive lineman. After graduation, he began coaching football—and working at a bank during the off-season. He eventually returned to coach at his alma mater and later moved on to coach at West Point. Lombardi's star began to rise further when the New York Giants hired him as an assistant coach. He coached there for five years and became renowned for his ability to diagram plays on the backboard, as well as for his fiery personality. He developed a reputation for valuing discipline, routine, and hard work—but also for doing things differently than they had been done before.[2]

While he was with the Giants, Lombardi introduced some of his innovative ideas and experiments that eventually began to add up and make the team more successful. One of those was rethinking how offensive linemen blocked their opponents. Up to that point, the best practice was to assign every offensive lineman a player on the defense to block. Lombardi wanted a more dynamic approach; he wanted his players to block opportunistically based on how the offensive play developed. The players would call their own blocks based on what they saw.[3] Another great example was how Lombardi used technology to gain an edge on his opponents. While the practice of watching game film had been in place for several years, Lombardi took things a step further when he had the Giants owner, Wellington Mara, take instant Polaroid shots of how the opposing team was lining up during the game. Mara would then place the photos in a weighted sock—which was attached to a guy line that connected Mara's booth with the sideline—and send the shots to Lombardi.[4] The coach would then make adjustments in the game based on what he was seeing—a practice that is now commonplace in today's modern game.

In 1959 the Giants had become one of the best teams in the league. At the same time, the Packers were one of the worst—and they were on the hunt for a new coach to turn their fortunes around. That led them to Lombardi—who, at the age of forty-five, was considered a bit old to be chosen as a rookie head coach. Most of the local sportswriters were pushing the team to hire one of its former coaches. And yet, the Packers' decision-makers believed Lombardi was "an innovative strategist and dynamic leader who believed in discipline."[5] Even then, it was a bold choice. Little did they know that by bucking the norm within the league, they would end up changing the game of football as a result of their counter-intuitive hire.

When Lombardi kicked off the first training camp with his new team, he made it clear he was going to do things differently than the team was used to—one step at a time. He didn't have a grand plan for them. Rather, his goal, in his words, was to "throw out the garbage." He wanted to simplify everything about how the team played the game and even rethink which players best fit which positions. He wanted to experiment and see what worked—and what didn't. At that first meeting, he told the players: "Gentlemen, we have a great deal of ground to cover. We're going to do things a lot differently than they've been done here before." He went on to say: "We're going to relentlessly chase perfection, knowing full well we will not catch it, because perfection is not attainable. But we are going to relentlessly chase it because, in the process, we will catch excellence . . . I'm not remotely interested in being just good."[6]

Lombardi's words stunned his players—but he made his point. Lombardi's team was going to do things differently, one step at a time, experimenting with new ways to beat the competition. He wanted his team to be the best, which is very different than being perfect. The game of football hasn't been the same since.

PERFECTION IS NOT THE POINT

Most people who visited my office and saw Vince Lombardi's "chasing perfection" quote hanging above my desk assumed that perfection was my ultimate goal. But they were wrong. It is important to read the whole quote. It says that perfection is unattainable, and I believe it's also overrated. If the goal isn't perfection, then what is it? It's knowing there is always a better way. We were striving for excellence at Cree, to do something that had never been done before. Today's perfection is nothing more than tomorrow's opportunity for innovation.

At Cree, we had many of the best scientists in the world working on our biggest challenges. We were at our core a material sciences company trying to develop new material systems that would enable new types of semiconductor devices. We knew in theory that these new materials would have properties to enable devices to do things that were previously not possible. That sounds great, except that no one had ever been able to invent these materials. In our case, we were focused on silicon carbide, the third hardest material known to exist after diamond and another material you've likely never heard of (cubic boron nitride). You might have come across carbide-tipped saw blades at your local hardware store with a special extra hard coating to make them cut better. These are often made with an industrial version of silicon carbide that has existed for many years. This version is polycrystalline, which is good for cutting, but not useful as a semiconductor. We needed to make single-crystal silicon carbide—but nobody knew how to do this. What do you do when there are no experts to call?

What we did was take our best ideas and start trying things. This approach started many years ago when several of the Cree founders were studying at North Carolina State University. They worked in a lab that was being funded by the U.S. Navy to try and develop a way to make silicon carbide for future semiconductor applications. After their lab demonstrated a basic ability to make semiconductor-quality material, the technology was spun out of the university in 1987 and became the foundation for Cree. The challenge was that the tiny crystal they had demonstrated in the lab could not be repeatedly produced and was far too small to make a wafer of any size, let alone the four- or six-inch wafers that would be needed for any real applications. So they embarked on a thirty-year journey to figure it out. They had to develop their own machines, create the processes to run in the machines, and even invent some new physics along the way. When I joined the company in 1993, the team had spent six years trying new ideas, getting results, adjusting based on the new information, and trying the next thing. We had achieved the ability to make a one-and-three-sixteenths-inch wafer. You know that if you're measuring progress in sixteenths, you're a long way from the six-inch goal. Twenty-five years and countless experiments and learning later, Cree finally achieved the six-inch goal and is now on to the next size. They don't know exactly how, but as long as they keep learning and embrace the concept of directionally correct, I have no doubt they'll get there. The team at Cree took an idea that seemed impossible, and through a relentless quest to try the next thing, accomplished something the experts thought would never happen.

LEARNING BY DOING (AND NOT GIVING UP)

I mentioned earlier in the book that I'm six feet, six inches tall. As you can imagine, that can make shopping for clothes that fit well a challenge. That's how I became a fan of the clothing company Bonobos—which offers a unique model in which they have created many more clothing variations than a typical apparel company to enable a better fit. Bonobos combines clothing that really fits with the power of the internet to deliver it. It's a best-of-both-worlds situation. The Bonobos model has been such a success that other retailers are trying to replicate its approach. In 2017 Walmart spent a reported $310 million to acquire the brand (which is not sold in Walmart stores, but online through Walmart's jet.com business and on bonobos.com).[7]

It wasn't until I heard a podcast featuring Andy Dunn, one of Bonobos's cofounders, that I realized that the company's journey began with a willingness to just get started. The idea for the company came about when Dunn's roommate and classmate at Stanford Graduate School of Business, Brian Spaly, decided to pursue his passion for making men's khaki pants that fit better. The problem he was trying to solve was that men's pants were either too tight in the waist or in the thighs, the latter often resulting in a baggy seat. So he worked with a tailor to create new patterns, went out and bought a bunch of fabric, and then took all of that to a garment factory in San Francisco that could stitch him up a few dozen pairs of pants. Spaly then began selling those pants to his classmates for a hundred dollars a pop. He decided to name his fledgling brand Bonobos—after a species of ape. One night, Spaly and Dunn hosted a "pants party" at their apartment where they invited friends to come and try them out. They sold $60,000 in a single night— which was eye-opening to Dunn. But Bonobos was just a hobby for Spaly, who had landed a new job at a venture capital firm after graduation. For Dunn, however, he saw the chance to run Bonobos full-time—something Spaly agreed with. Then, if things really took off, Spaly could come back and join the company.[8]

The odds weren't in Dunn's favor. In 2007, when Bonobos.com launched, he had about $3,000 in the bank and some $60,000 in loans. He didn't really have a business model or a long-term plan.

He just wanted to test the idea that he could sell pants online—which was still a novel idea at the time. "I believed that if you could make a brand using a catalog, you could make bigger brands using the power of the web," he told podcast interviewer Guy Raz. "We are going to build this online, not brick and mortar. It was going to be Ralph Lauren plus Zappos."[9]

Dunn understood that if Bonobos was going to succeed with offering customizable clothes for consumers, it could never stock everything customers needed. It would require thousands of variations of every pant or shirt the company offered. So instead, he created a clothing store that actually had no clothing—a completely novel and innovative model that solved problems for the customer (they could get clothes that fit perfectly) and for the business (it didn't have to invest in inventory that nobody wanted). This model would eventually be the turning point for the company's fortunes.[10]

Dunn caught a break early on when a couple of his professors from Stanford, who were also venture capitalists, agreed to invest a combined $300,000 in his business—which he promptly used to move to New York City. There, Dunn began peddling his pants one referral at a time until, one day, the company caught a huge break when it got featured on a prominent blog. Dunn then got a call from his lone employee, who said, "Andy, we're getting too many orders. Should I shut the site down?"[11] Bonobos was now on the map—but the journey was only just beginning.

As sales at the company soared, just about doubling every month until they hit the $1 million mark at the end of the first year, Spaly came back to the company. He took over a lot of the product-related work while Dunn, as CEO, focused more on issues related to hiring, marketing, and fundraising since the company was still burning cash. But the two friends and business partners soon ran into conflict with each other in terms of who made decisions about the direction of the business—a falling out that led Spaly to leave the company in 2008. It was an emotional breakup for Dunn, who realized that he could no longer blame anyone else for issues the company was running into. "There was a battle for the soul of the company," Dunn said. "We couldn't decide if we were a menswear company or a tech company."[12] Dunn also admitted to making mistakes both in the people he hired and in the decision to open a second office in California—which he later closed—knowing the company would lose many of its software engineers in the process. He told Guy Raz on the podcast:

> I was really scared. What I learned in eleven years of doing this was that sometimes you're most afraid when you're making the most important decisions. If it's not scary, then it's not hard. I learned what we have to value more is courage . . . I was defiant in the face of a terrifying reality. Ultimately you have to believe; it's faith. Companies don't die because they fail; it's because the entrepreneur gives up. Our goal was to keep the lights on, keep growing, and keep learning. And that's what we did.[13]

By 2014 the company had moved closer to breaking even. The paradox, however, was that the e-commerce side of the business was still losing money. It was the company's partnerships with brick-and-mortar retailers like Nordstrom that were keeping the company going. Even more successful were its Guideshops, a concept Bonobos launched in 2011 that offered no merchandise for sale. Rather, they were places where consumers could browse and get fitted for clothes that would then be shipped to their homes—a "fit-to-ship" model that other retailers scoffed at, saying it would never work. The traditional retailers said consumers are all about instant gratification, but it turns out they didn't know what consumers really wanted.

In an interview with *USA Today*, Dunn, in response to a question about what advice he would give to other entrepreneurs, said: "Focus on the product . . . and don't worry about the future. It may look in retrospect that everything is planned, but it wasn't at all. There was so much experimentation. You gotta have that belief in yourself that you are going to make it on your own."[14] That's someone who understood how to uncover their innovator's spirit.

HIGH-VOLUME INNOVATION

One of the early challenges at Cree was the scope of the problem we were taking on. Developing a new semiconductor material system, one that most experts think is not possible, is a daunting proposition—especially for a small start-up company. Had we fully understood the scale of the problem, how long it would take, and how much money we would eventually need, I don't know that we would have ever started down the path. I do know the early investors didn't fully appreciate what they were signing up for. But the founders had an important problem to solve and a vision that they could create real value—someday. So they embarked on the process of innovation, with a strategy of being directionally correct as their guide.

One of the challenges with this approach was that we needed a team of people who were comfortable with making constant adjustments based on what we were learning from the market. We also needed a lot of cycles of learning, which you get by running numerous experiments. In most larger companies, this means a dedicated R&D team operating in a dedicated R&D facility. We couldn't afford two facilities in the early days, so we adopted the idea of running production and R&D on the same lines at the same time—something that was unheard of to most industry people. We also believed that learning was the most important factor to our future success, so we decided that we would run R&D seven days a week, twenty-four hours a day—just like production.

Our approach to high-volume innovation was driven by the desire for high-volume learning. We estimated that we were running ten to twenty times more experiments in a week than any of our competitors. Admittedly, it made for a messy environment and we sacrificed production yields due to the constant experimenting, but it allowed us to learn on the fly and move quickly. It also solved the problem of transferring a new product from R&D to production. Our approach also allowed us to bring new products to market much faster, gaining insight from our customers to make additional changes that would then make the products even better. We had prioritized learning over perfection.

To be clear, this concept was not the result of some grand strategy. Rather, it was the product of necessity. What do you do when you have a disadvantage in scale and resources? Turn it into an advantage of speed and innovation. I didn't fully appreciate our advantage until a manufacturing expert from a large Japanese company visited our factory. As I toured him through our production line, I could tell that he was surprised at what he saw. The idea that we would run production and R&D simultaneously, while constantly making changes in our quest for better products, challenged just about every accepted belief he had about how to run a semiconductor factory and optimize efficiency and quality.

After the tour, the Japanese executive came up to me and smiled. He said it could often take more than a year for their team to move a product from R&D into production and we had simply eliminated the transfer. He also commented that with our unique approach, he could see that our rate of learning was many times higher than what they could achieve. That's how we moved faster than our competitors. We had optimized our business for innovation, because we weren't willing to wait for perfection.

BUILD-MEASURE-LEARN

Being directionally correct and not waiting for perfection came naturally to the founders of Cree, and we took their approach and scaled it to build a large innovation company. A number of years ago, I described this concept to a colleague who said that it sounded a lot like the agile development approach. At the time, I honestly hadn't heard of agile development. But after doing some research, I realized that someone had come along and given a name to what Cree and other companies had been doing for years. The *Manifesto for Agile Software Development* was published in 2001 by a group of seventeen software developers.[15] The concept is based on trying to learn as you go rather than trying to execute against a grand plan that might never work out. The idea was further refined by a Silicon Valley software veteran named Eric Ries, who in 2008 coined the phrase "The Lean Startup" (and later published a book of the same name) to describe how he and his cofounders used the principles of agile development to build their company, IMVU. The concept for building companies this way is based on the notion of "build-measure-learn." Ries writes: "The fundamental activity of a startup is to turn ideas into products, measure how customers respond, and then learn whether to pivot or persevere. All successful startup processes should be geared to accelerate that feedback loop."[16] He also writes that start-ups, by their very nature, exist to learn.

This approach is now commonplace, especially in Silicon Valley. Rather than strive for perfection before they hit the market, companies are now testing their products with imperfections and letting the market help them refine their products. While learning is critical, by itself it does not lead to innovation.

EXPERIMENTATION IS NOT INNOVATION

Experimentation and rapidly testing new ideas has been embraced by most, if not all, of the major tech companies who have come to dominate our lives. According to Google, the company has been able to remain on the cutting edge by embracing its "Eight Pillars of Innovation." For example, one of Google's pillars is "Think big but start small," which its website describes as "no matter how ambitious the plan, you have to roll up your sleeves and start somewhere."[17] Another Google pillar is "Launch early and iterate," which is quite similar to the principles of the lean start-up method, but let's not worry about who deserves the credit. The point is that agility or nimbleness is a powerful tool for innovation. I agree with this concept. But I believe that the tools have become the focus of these organizations, instead of the mindset that really drives innovation.

Let's test this with the question of whether Google is truly innovative. I think most people would say yes. But as I mentioned in an earlier chapter, I'm skeptical when companies start marketing their innovation prowess—and this looks like marketing to me. I have no doubt that Google built its expertise in search and online advertising through innovation. And I know the company is constantly experimenting with new ideas in areas that include self-driving cars, robotics, artificial intelligence, 3-D mapping, smart contact lenses, and even immortality. But experimenting without purpose, without solving a problem and creating value, is not innovation. It's just experimenting. So, what's missing? The drive to find a way—the will to win.

Google is proud of the fact that not every project it started succeeded. It openly describes its willingness to kill a project as a strength. It's great that the company is unafraid of failure, but is it driven to succeed? Look at recent examples like Google Inbox and Google+, the company's failed attempt to enter the social media arena—could these have succeeded if the future of the company depended on it? By one recent count, Google now has some 158 failed projects over its twenty-year history—something that some observers see as completely wasteful.[18] I think these critics miss the point, as I don't think we should ever consider learning to be wasteful, but I don't see where these projects have led to innovations. For example, why is Google developing a driverless car?[19] I have no doubt that they employ some of the smartest people on the planet and that they could build a great driverless car—if it was required for the company to survive. But I doubt they will. Why? Because they don't have to. Google is built on ads and the company will go on whether or not the car project succeeds.

I believe that Google is falling into a similar trap that R&D labs like Xerox PARC and Bell Labs fell victim to: They disconnected invention from the need to solve a problem. Steve Jobs, on a visit to the Xerox labs, saw a demonstration of the mouse and graphical user interface they had created and later turned it into a real innovation as part of the Apple line of computers.[20] It took someone like Jobs—whose company was at an early make-or-break point at the time—to make it work because he couldn't afford not to. As long as Google can afford not to succeed, I think it will struggle to convert its inventions into innovations.

Experimentation and iteration are powerful tools that can lead to innovation. But innovation requires much more than testing your ideas. Innovation requires purpose, drive, and focus to overcome the obstacles that will inevitably get in the way of solving a problem and creating value. It is a mindset that makes you keep going when others would give up. That's why you often need the kind of focus that comes from crisis to succeed.

CHAPTER ELEVEN RECAP

Belief: It's better to make a decision with what you know, learn from it, and move forward.

Behavior: Don't wait for perfection.

KEY INSIGHTS

Embrace directionally correct. 1) Pick a direction; 2) Take your best idea; 3) Try it and see what happens; and 4) Use what you learned to adjust and try again.

Chase excellence. You just have to start. In the process of chasing perfection, you will achieve excellence.

Experimentation is not innovation. Experimenting without purpose, without solving a problem and creating value, is just experimenting.

CHAPTER TWELVE

Focus the Mind

*"Concentrate all your thoughts upon the work at hand.
The sun's rays do not burn until brought to a focus."*
—Alexander Graham Bell

THINK OF AN EXAMPLE OF a really hard problem that you tried to solve, but you just couldn't figure it out. Why did you give up? If you knew that the fate of your career (or your company) depended on you finding a solution, is there something else you might have tried? It's been my experience that when your back is up against the wall, the innovator's spirit truly flourishes because it brings about an incredible sense of focus—especially in a multitasking anti-focused world littered with distractions. Focus is an extremely powerful tool that can give ordinary people the ability to do the extraordinary. That's especially true when people's lives are literally at stake.

FAILURE IS NOT AN OPTION

On the evening of Monday, April 11, 1970, three astronauts sitting atop a giant rocket blasted off into space on their way to the moon. But two days later, as the crew of *Apollo* 13 hurtled thousands of miles an hour through space, disaster struck—one of the spacecraft's oxygen tanks exploded, causing the other to fail. The cause was a faulty wire that had been overlooked amid all the countless hours spent preparing the spacecraft and crew for their mission. Everything inside the craft had multiple redundant parts—that's why there were two tanks. But no one ever imagined that both tanks could fail at the same time.

The oxygen was combined with hydrogen to power the craft's three fuel cells, which would generate the electricity, air, and water the crew needed for their mission. Now, thanks to the explosion, there was limited power and they were literally running out of clean air to breathe. The astronauts' lives were in peril—as were their chances of returning safely to Earth. The only hope they had was for the Mission Control team back in Houston to figure out a way to keep them alive while getting them on a course where they could safely crash back into one of Earth's oceans. The stakes were enormous, and the entire planet tuned in to watch what happened. Henry S. F. Cooper Jr., author of *Thirteen: The Apollo Flight That Failed*, writes: "The *Apollo* 13 astronauts were now in every bit as understandable and distressing a predicament as seamen aboard a leaky vessel in danger of foundering. This was readily grasped by the estimated third of the world's population who were following *Apollo* 13—probably more than had followed any other spaceflight."[1]

It was a true life-or-death crisis.

For the next four days, the three astronauts—James "Jim" Lovell, Fred Haise, and John "Jack" Swigert—would be pushed to the limits of their mental and physical endurance as they tried to keep their spacecraft flying based on instructions they received from Mission Control. There were checklists upon checklists to implement, which grew increasingly difficult for the astronauts to follow as the lack of sleep, water, and heat eroded their mental faculties (their kidneys began to fail as well). At the same time, the dozens of scientists back on Earth were being pushed to their limits trying to find solutions to the problems at hand—to a situation no one had ever anticipated.

Swigert would later write: "Nobody thought the spacecraft would lose two fuel cells and two oxygen tanks. It couldn't happen. If somebody had thrown that at us in the simulator, we'd have said, 'Come on, you're not being realistic.'"[2] But it had happened, and now it was literally a situation of innovate or die.

The Mission Control team, including several fellow astronauts, rallied around the *Apollo* crew. They split into multiple teams, each focused on different problems but working together under the direction of famed flight director Eugene "Gene" Kranz. They needed to find ways to keep the astronauts alive with whatever power and air the ship had left. And, unlike past space missions, where they could basically work directly from their procedure, they had to come up with something entirely new. Cooper writes: "A number of things would have to be done that had never been done before."

That included finding ways to innovate and improvise on the fly. A scene from the movie *Apollo 13* starring Tom Hanks shows how a team of NASA engineers found a way to rig up an adapter for a carbon dioxide scrubber out of whatever parts the astronauts would have on hand. In another case, engineers devised a way to have the circuits inside the craft redirect power to keep critical functions working using a method that had never been attempted or simulated before (fortunately, it worked).

The team focused on reentry needed to find a way to have the astronauts splash down in a part of the world where rescue ships would be able to quickly get to them—while also avoiding a deadly hurricane on the move. That team was also responsible for creating the checklist the astronauts needed to copy down manually and follow—something that typically had as many pages as an old-fashioned telephone book. Normally, that checklist would take three months to nail down. Now, they had to create one in less than three days—while working within the constraints of severely limited power and water supplies.

In what proved to be an inspiring story of focus and innovation, the Mission Control team, working in tandem with the increasingly frail astronauts, somehow found a way to get them home. As the crew of the nearby aircraft carrier USS *Iwo Jima* looked on, the *Apollo* 13 command module's parachutes deployed and helped the craft splash safely down in the Pacific Ocean on April 17. You can imagine the cheers that erupted around the world, especially within Mission Control.

Kranz, who retained a sense of eerie calm throughout the incident and would later write a book of his own called *Failure Is Not an Option,* said at the time: "In our preparations, we never believed we couldn't get the men back. I thought that as a group we were smart enough, and clever enough, to get out of the problem."[3] The astronauts were saved thanks to the efforts of a team of incredible innovators who put all of their focus into a single goal: getting their guys home.

It's an incredible story. It's also a great lesson in how a crisis can help generate the kind of focus innovators need to push the envelope. A crisis gives you license to eliminate distractions as a way to ensure that everyone pushes toward the goal in a way that makes failure not an option.

So, is crisis good for innovation? Or is it bad? I remember attending a Strategic Leadership Forum event in November 2010 in Palm Desert, California. Bill Ford, the executive chairman of Ford Motor Company, was being interviewed by Charlie Rose about the company's rise from the verge of bankruptcy in 2008. Ford recounted the story of how he had to convince his family members, who controlled almost forty percent of the company voting shares, to allow him to pledge the trademarked blue Ford oval, his family name, as collateral for a financing package to help the company survive the Great Recession. He commented that, prior to the financial crisis, he had been working for several years without much success to try and focus the company on making great cars instead of being mired in internal politics and infighting. But mortgaging the family legacy in the face of bankruptcy created a focus that allowed the company to break through these decades-old barriers and make real changes under the guidance of new CEO Alan Mullaly. As I listened to this story, I realized something that I had experienced many times, but never before put into words: that a crisis creates an environment for innovation by focusing everyone on the real problem at hand.

FOCUS DRIVES INNOVATION

The development of the Cree LED light bulb, which I mentioned in several previous chapters, is a lesson in using focus to drive innovation. In the spring of 2012, Gerry (the same long-bearded scientist) stopped by my office with Neal Hunter (who was now working with the lighting group) and said they wanted to show me something. I had heard that Gerry had been working on a new product concept called "Phil," but until that point I had no idea what it was. Phil turned out to be a prototype of an LED light bulb.

This was quite surprising to me for two reasons. First, we had discussed making an LED bulb in the past but had decided it was not a business we should be in. I had clearly communicated both internally and externally that Cree wasn't going to make an LED bulb. But that hadn't stopped Gerry. He was sick of waiting for the other lighting companies to figure it out, so he decided to solve the problem and make one on his own (a sign of an innovator). Second, the prototype was incredible. It looked and worked just like a regular light bulb, and the team believed it could be sold for less than $10 (a key retail price point to get consumers to try something new). Prior to this point, the few LED bulbs on the market were very "high-tech looking"—which is a code name for weird—and were much more expensive. Up to that point, consumers had not been motivated to try the new technology.

We knew that day we were looking at the future. And I knew that if we tried to bring this concept to market within our large lighting business, it would fail.

Why did I think that? At this point, Cree was a $1 billion company with lots of processes, managers, and bureaucracy to help drive more predictable results. I knew those same processes and managers would kill any chance we had of getting this product to market. So we did what you would do if you don't want a large organization getting in the way of innovation: We didn't tell anyone.

We were going to develop the LED bulb in secret at a new location that we would rent for just this purpose. The original five-person team was not to tell anybody where they were going or what they were doing. If asked, they were to simply say they were working on a new R&D project. They would be disconnected from the rest of the company and completely focused on their goal. No distractions. Their mission was to take this prototype, turn it into a product, and bring it to market within a year. They had leeway to break any rules they needed to reach their goal (as long as it was legal, ethical, and good for the company), and this team had shown the ability to be good at ignoring rules in the past. We told them not to come back unless they succeeded. There was no backup plan—they had to find a way.

We did this because we knew that big innovations are exciting, but they can also be distracting to the rest of the company. We had a rule: Unless someone could add value to solving a core problem faced by the innovation team, there was no point in having those people involved.

Within the year, that team of innovators developed the world's first commercially successful LED light bulb—which put the Cree brand on the map. They faced many obstacles along the way, but they adapted and kept going. The team had to develop a production line to make these bulbs, which required inventing several new processes and machines. They had to find a customer, which eventually they did in The Home Depot, who were convinced to take a chance on a small company that had never before made a consumer product.

Most of the company remained in the dark about the project until the day it was announced in April 2013 via our first TV commercial aired during the National Basketball Association playoffs. We launched the bulb in all two thousand Home Depot stores, and although it looked a little different from that first prototype I saw, it was a true innovation. While a few people at Cree questioned why they hadn't been involved in the project, they were drowned out by the celebration around the company. Together, we had invented a better light bulb that would change lighting forever. And the "we" included everyone in the company, not just the original five who took on the task in secret.

I feel confident that none of this would have ever happened if we hadn't chosen the right group of people to form this team and created an environment with very limited distractions. The difference between innovation success and failure often comes down to focus and the will to win.

BURN THE BOATS

Ideally your team of innovators is unafraid of failure, but sometimes doubt creeps into a team. So what do you do? If you really want a team to focus on the task at hand and commit to a difficult goal, raise the stakes by removing any kind of backup plan. In his book, *The Art of War*, Sun Tzu, the ancient Chinese general and philosopher, quotes another general, Tu Mu, who said: "When your army has crossed the border, you should burn your boats and bridges, in order to make it clear to everybody that you have no hankering after home."[4] Sun Tzu adds his own context: "Throw the troops into a position from which there is no escape and even when faced with death they will not flee. . . . Then officers and men together put forth their utmost efforts. In a desperate situation they fear nothing; when there is no way out they stand firm."[5]

While it's doubtful he read Sun Tzu, Spanish conquistador Hernán Cortés used that tactic during his invasion of Mexico in 1520. Once his troops were ashore, Cortés ordered them to strip everything of value from the ships—from the metalwork to the sails—and then, rather than burn his boats, he had the ships sunk or scuttled offshore. He is reported to have said that he left his men with "nothing to rely on save their own hands—and the certainty that they must either win the land or die in the attempt."

I know these are military examples, but there's an important lesson that can be applied to innovation—namely, how you can create intense focus when you take away a fallback plan. While it might seem comforting to know that you have a Plan B if Plan A doesn't work out, that can actually backfire in terms of creating the kind of focus you need to reach whatever innovation goal you are striving for.

Consider the story that Jim Collins, the famed business researcher and author of iconic books like *Good to Great*, told Tim Ferriss during an interview on Ferriss's podcast. Before he became a world-famous author, Collins was a professor at Stanford University. But he was considering leaving his job to go research and write his book *Built to Last*. Collins said that up to that point he had been "firing bullets" for six to seven years to help calibrate the direction of his career. But now, he was considering loading up all of his gunpowder and firing a "cannonball"—what he equated with an all-in effort to tackle something (he also called it a "Thelma and Louise" moment, named for the movie of the same name where two women drive their car off a cliff).

But before he took such a dramatic step, he went to his mentors at the university and asked them if he should try not to burn any bridges at Stanford so he could come back if the book didn't work out. While that might seem like a reasonable position to take for many of us, Collins's mentor disagreed. He told him that "an option to come back has negative value on the creative path." In other words, said Collins, "If you have the option to come back, it will change your behavior. You have to go all in 100 percent, otherwise you'll hold something in reserve, and when it gets really scary, you'll pull back. The option to come back is not in your best interest. . . . You have to find a way to get to the other side."[6] Or, to say that yet another way, the best way to innovate is to seal off your ability to retreat. That's how you create focus.

In many ways, I feel like this is what the movie subscription service Netflix did when it made the switch from offering DVDs through the mail to offering online streaming subscriptions back in 2011. While watching an old-fashioned DVD might seem quaint now (I'm not sure I even have a way to watch one anymore), Netflix had built a multibillion-dollar public company on its once unique ability to ship movies to customers through the mail. But Reed Hastings, the company's cofounder and CEO, realized that the future was online. Not only had competitors like Walmart, Amazon, and Redbox sprung up, but it was also becoming more difficult for Netflix to get access to the newest or best movies released by the studios. Plus, broadband internet was getting faster and cheaper while at the same time postage costs were increasing. Going 100 percent online would give Netflix the ability to do something new: create its own content, which would only be available to its subscribers. And to do that, it began to invest millions in making the switch.[7]

It was a bold bet—and it seemed to backfire early on. When Netflix announced that it was splitting off its DVD rental business (calling it Qwikster) and raising its subscription price from $10 to $16 a month, the backlash was furious. A reported eight hundred thousand people canceled their subscriptions over the next three months, causing the company's stock to plunge from $300 a share to just $65 a share.[8] While the company hadn't completely burned its boats, it had certainly launched the cannonball that would make or break its fortunes. Said Ted Sarandos, the head of content at Netflix: "We never spent one minute trying to save the DVD business."[9] There was no turning back at that point.

Creating that sense of focus made sure everyone inside the company knew what the stakes were. The secret to Netflix's return to glory turned out to be its original content, such as the shows *House of Cards* and *Orange Is the New Black*, both of which debuted in 2013 and proved to be incredibly popular. (Which wasn't a complete surprise to the team at Netflix, since they had analyzed the viewing patterns of their subscribers to find a match they thought lots of viewers would love—their version of calibrating by firing bullets.)[10] Entire seasons of the shows were released all at once, basically creating the phenomenon we now call binge-watching. New subscribers began to sign up by the thousands, and soon, the company's stock price was back on the rise.

THE MOTIVATING POWER OF RIVALRIES

Have you ever had a rival in your life? Maybe it was someone you competed against in sports growing up—or even someone in the classroom you were always trying to get better grades than. What was the effect on your motivation? This probably dates me somewhat, but it's been said that the rivalry between the Beatles and the Beach Boys propelled each band to new levels of creativity in their songwriting. The point is that rivals can actually force us to focus our efforts in really interesting ways. A group of researchers have studied this phenomenon extensively, especially on how it affects things like our willingness to take risks.[11] In one case, the researchers studied the impact that playing a rival has on National Football League teams. They found that when teams played a key division rival, they were much more likely to take risks by, say, going for it on fourth down or attempting a two-point conversion after a touchdown rather than kicking the relatively risk-free extra point.

The researchers performed a similar experiment on college students who were told they were going to be evaluated on their decision-making skills compared to those of students from a rival university—think about a North Carolina Tar Heel pitted against a Duke Blue Devil (or when the Packers play the Bears). Yet again, they found that the participants were more willing to take risks— perhaps in part because going against a rival was shown to increase the student's heart rate. Apparently, we literally get pumped up to beat a rival.

But perhaps just as interesting is that the researchers examined whether the participants exhibited what they called a promotion focus mindset, where a person is more focused on achieving an ideal outcome, or whether they were drawn to a mindset of prevention focus, or avoiding negative outcomes. The researchers found that when going up against a rival, people are much more likely to focus on achieving an ideal outcome. As a runner, that might mean ringing in a best time because you don't hold anything back when matched up against your rival. But the same kind of thing can happen in a business as well.

The researchers wrote about the implications of their findings in an article for the *Harvard Business Review*:

> In organizations and industries in which experimentation, innovation, bold strategic moves, and thinking outside the box are valued (e.g., technology), rivalry could be an important lever for managers to pull to incentivize risk-taking. This could mean emphasizing longstanding corporate rivalries, or fostering (friendly) rivalries between employees, perhaps by creating incentive systems that provide for repeated competitions (of course, there are risks to doing this that should also be considered).[12]

In a separate article for *Entrepreneur* magazine, one of the researchers, Gavin Kilduff, a professor at New York University's Stern School of Business, said that rivalries can be particularly effective between organizations. As the article states: "For most businesses, identifying a competitor and then focusing on outperforming them can increase motivation and identification within the organization."[13]

An interesting wrinkle to Kilduff's research is that he makes the distinction between competition and rivalry. He defines competition as any situation in which the goals or outcomes of the actors involved are opposed to one another. So a gain for one player inherently comes at a loss for the other. But rivalry is more personal; it's built on relationships. "We're discovering more and more that having someone you are a little competitive with, who you compare your progress to, can be a very motivating force," Kilduff said.[14]

That hits home for me. As I mentioned earlier in the book, my brother Mark also happened to work in the LED industry. This interesting twist of family dynamics created a friendly rivalry that helped create a sense of focus for the team at Cree. Mark was the head of sales at Lumileds, who was a competitor. Cree was the new player in the market; they were one of the established leaders in the industry. This dynamic led to plenty of brotherly banter (more like trash-talking) between us over which company's LEDs were better. When people found out that we were brothers and competitors, they would often ask: What it's like when you get together over the holidays? I would usually just laugh it off.

First and foremost, we were brothers. We didn't let work come between us. But that didn't mean that we didn't enjoy a friendly rivalry as well. One of the things my brother had been doing for a couple of years at family get-togethers, for instance, was to show off a flashlight with his company's LEDs so everyone could see how bright it was. One year he even gave us all (my sisters, parents, and myself included) a Christmas gift of Lumileds's latest flashlight. He commented to me, "Where's your flashlight?" The implication was that the Lumileds flashlight was better and brighter than anything Cree could make and that's why I didn't have one. Later that year, I decided I had had enough, and it was time to put my brother in his place.

My family and I were flying out to California to spend Thanksgiving with Mark and his family. Cree had just launched the XLamp LED, but it had yet to take off in the market. So I went to Gerry, the same guy with the ZZ Top beard, and explained the situation. I showed him the Lumileds flashlight and I asked him if he could help me blow my brother away by making something brighter. I needed to win the unofficial family holiday brightest LED competition. (I know that sounds like something only two engineers would care about, but it was important.) Gerry smiled and said, "I've got you covered." What he did was take apart the flashlight my brother had previously given me as a gift and replace their LED with one of our new XLamp LEDs. We tested it and it was awesome. Gerry's measurement said our flashlight was more than twice as bright. The trap was set.

Sometime after we got to California, I casually asked my brother if he had a new flashlight to show off. He got excited and said he did—after which he produced one with their latest LEDs. (I should note that at this point our wives were thinking this is ridiculous—but there was no stopping us.) He shined his flashlight on the wall and it was pretty good. I told him that I also had a flashlight. His eyebrows went up. "Oh yeah?" he said. "Let me see what it can do." We then shined both lights on the wall to compare them—and mine totally blew his away. He seemed stunned, but then when he saw the flashlight he said, "Hey, that's the flashlight I gave you!" I told him he was right, but now it had a Cree LED in it. "Let me see that," he said. "Sorry," I said. "I can't show it to you; it's proprietary."

And with that, I won the first-ever Swoboda Flashlight Competition—and Cree would go on to dominate the LED flashlight category for the next five years. It's amazing how much a rivalry can help drive innovation.

UNLEASH THE UNDERDOGS

When you're building a team of innovators, where do you look for the best team members? It is often not where you might expect. Earlier in the book, I talked about how Pixar, the incredibly successful animation studio, embraced the brutal truths when it came to pushing new ideas and concepts. It turns out Pixar was also good at something else: unleashing its misfits. In his podcast *WorkLife*, Adam Grant, an organizational psychologist, dug into how Pixar wound up making the phenomenally successful 2004 movie *The Incredibles*, which featured a family of superheroes.[15] It's a great movie if you haven't seen it, regardless of how old you are. Grant found out that, although Pixar was at the top of its game at the time, they were worried about resting on their laurels. The leaders at Pixar hired Brad Bird, a director whose animated movie *The Iron Giant* had bombed at the box office, because they liked how Bird's movie was different and they wanted to see if he could come up with something innovative.

Rather than tackle that effort alone, Bird recruited other supposedly disgruntled and "misfit" workers at Pixar, or, as they eventually called themselves, "pirates"—people whose ideas and creativity had been marginalized by others inside the company. Bird was giving them the chance to do something different—something that would be uniquely theirs. He told Grant:

> There's a big impetus, especially with success, to repeat whatever has worked before. You know: if it ain't broke, don't fix it. But I was looking for a bunch of people that were kind of dissatisfied with the way things were. . . . I want people who are disgruntled because they have a better way of doing things and they are having trouble finding an avenue. Racing cars that are just spinning their wheels in a garage rather than racing. You open that garage and, man, those people take you somewhere.[16]

But Bird also employed an additional piece of motivational strategy on his team to inspire them to complete the movie: He told them that nobody else thought they could pull it off. According to one member of his team, Bird got up on a table and told the crew: "They think we can't do this. They think we're too slow. They think we're not good enough. . . . I tell you we're going to do this!" It was a very intentional strategy on Bird's part to get the team to focus on their goal—and to prove to the others within the company that they could do it. Bird told Grant:

> One thing that is very effective is to find a common enemy. But the enemy doesn't have to be a person. It can be a mindset. It can be a presumption. It can be a system that doesn't want to change. It can even be some-thing like a trend in movies that is just making movies stupider. You can make that the enemy, and you can put

it up in front of people and say, "You know what I don't like? I don't like X, and here's how I think we can not do this thing that everyone is doing and really dazzle the audience." And people like that, because you're—you're putting them on the pirate ship. You know, you're not going with the well-funded safe routes. You're kind of striking your sails in a storm and you're okay with it. And that fires people up. It fires me up![17]

Grant points out that this dynamic is similar to what you find in people who consider themselves underdogs, or people who are fighting against the odds. As he defines it, an underdog is "a mindset that can help you approach problems the way black sheep do. You can position people as underdogs by telling them they're not expected to succeed. And surprisingly, the uphill battle is often the one that people are most excited to fight."[18] In other words, when someone feels like an underdog, they get amped up to prove the doubters wrong (a theme we explored back in Chapter Eight)—especially if it's someone they consider a rival. That's how telling someone they can't do something can actually become the fuel for innovation.

The result of telling this crew of misfit underdog pirates at Pixar that they couldn't do it was that they tried things no animators had pulled off before—such as filming an actual swimming pool or using a pie plate to serve as a flying saucer. Most animated movies at the time didn't feature humans, who are very hard to animate. The team tackled that challenge with relish, finding ways to use simple shapes like ovals to simulate human movements.[19] One of the ways Bird got the team to focus on their goal of making an innovative movie was to put animators together with the technical engineers in the same room—something they were the first to do.

The end result? *The Incredibles* became a blockbuster success, grossing more than $600 million at the box office and winning two Oscars.[20] It might also have permanently changed how animated movies are made going forward.

Whether it comes from a crisis, rivalry, or self-imposed secret innovation team, having a focused mind is an important element for innovation success.

But we're still left with one last unanswered question—the one we started with at the start of this book. How many barbers are there in New York City?

CHAPTER TWELVE RECAP

Belief: If you make success the only option, innovation will follow.

Behavior: Focus the mind.

KEY INSIGHTS

Crisis brings focus. When failure is not an option, especially during a crisis, innovators can accomplish amazing things.

Burn the boats. Backup plans can actually hurt innovation—they have negative value. Burning your boats and committing to go all in is an effective way to ignite innovation.

Rivalries are powerful motivators. Rivalries create an increased focus and willingness to take risks that lead the innovation.

The Journey Continues

CONGRATULATIONS! YOU HAVE COMPLETED THE first step in uncovering your innovator's spirit. I hope I've helped you challenge your beliefs and given you a picture of the behaviors that drive innovation. If it feels like you spent a long day interviewing at Cree, don't be deterred. Innovation is hard work. If you're excited about taking these ideas and applying them to a problem, then you are on your way to leading innovation. Don't overthink this. I've shown you what it looks like and hopefully you've discovered the courage to make the impossible possible. You can do it. It's time for you to find a problem worth solving and get started.

But first, we need to complete some unfinished business. Have you come up with an answer to how many barbers there are in New York? If yes, that's great. If no, it's not too late. Either way, here is how I would go about trying to come up with an answer.

I'd start with how many people live in the city. At last count, it's a little over eight million people. Then I'd figure out how many of those people might go to a barber. I assume that, in general, men go to barbers and women don't. So that reduces the number in half. Of course, some percentage of those men are either too young, too bald, or just don't go to a barber. So I would reduce the number by another fifty percent. That drops the total number of people who might go to the barber to about two million people.

So how many barbers would you need for two million customers? I would start with how long it takes to get a haircut. Based on my experience, I'd say the average is about thirty minutes, or two haircuts an hour. If a barber works the typical forty hours a week and has paying customers for about eighty percent of that time, that equates to about thirty-two hours of time cutting hair. Thirty-two hours at two haircuts per hour adds up to sixty-four haircuts a week.

Now, how often do people get their hair cut? It's probably about once every four weeks. That means an average barber can give about two hundred and fifty-six haircuts every four weeks (sixty-four multiplied by four). When you divide two million by two hundred and fifty-six, you come up with just under eight thousand barbers in New York City.

What's remarkable is that when I've asked people to try and answer this question, most of them have come up with an answer in the same ballpark. Is that actually how many barbers there are in New York City? I don't know. I've never spent the time to try and look it up. Once I calculated my estimate, I was satisfied that it was directionally correct and moved on to the next challenge. The point is to have the curiosity to want to know and the confidence to try and figure it out. This is the first step in the journey to discover your innovator's spirit. It starts with the belief that you can find a way to solve a problem no one else could.

Keep in mind that the innovator's spirit is not a recipe—it is a mindset. It's a set of beliefs that enable you to embrace the behaviors that lead to innovation. The belief that you don't manage innovation, you lead it. That it's not about best practice, it's about finding a better practice. That it's not about thinking outside the box, it's about setting the box on fire. And most important, that innovation is about people.

The innovator's spirit is critical to helping you stay motived in the face of failures, which will happen along the way. It will help you see failure as an opportunity to learn, as fuel for innovation. And it will give you the courage not only to do what others think you can't, but also to do what is right when those around you are rooting against you. Because one of the biggest barriers to letting your innovator's spirit flourish can be those around you who are invested in protecting the status quo. Their mindset is to protect their role, to protect what they have achieved. Imagine what the dynamic was like inside that room, for example, when I asked my question about the barbers. How do you think the people who laughed off my challenge felt when they saw that other people actually worked to come up with an answer? They probably felt resentful, right? Now, imagine what it might be like inside an organization when someone decides to take a risk and try out something new—to try to innovate. I saw this on many occasions, but it was disguised as a question. An innovative idea would be proposed, but quickly the feedback was "How do you know this will work?" or "Do you have data or research to back this up?" These questions sound reasonable, but they're often just a defense mechanism. You are trying to innovate and have a new idea, something that has never been done before. Sometimes you just have to believe and try. You can't be afraid to fail.

I share this with you because it's important to understand that as you continue your journey to fully embrace your innovator's spirit, it's imperative that you stay true to the beliefs and their connected behaviors that we discussed in this book. You can't give up in the face of the barriers you encounter—both in terms of innovating but also in terms of the doubters, cynics, and skeptics who will inevitably try to bar your way forward. Don't let them stop you. It's part of the process, and it makes getting to your goal all the more rewarding. Combining the will to win with the belief that there is always a way to get to the goal is how you make the impossible possible.

Now, stop reading and start doing. Go change the world!

Author's Note

WHILE THIS BOOK IS ABOUT you, about finding your innovator's spirit, it is also about the people around you. My approach to innovation is about improving the odds for innovation success. It requires finding people (either through hiring or recruiting from within your own organization) with the innovator's spirit. And then you want to increase the number of experiments (or bets you make). That combination will greatly improve the likelihood that you will achieve something new that solves a real problem and creates value.

So how do you find these people? Over the past twelve chapters, I posed about one hundred questions designed to help you uncover your innovator's spirit. Not all are designed to be asked in an actual interview, but many of them you could consider asking someone before they join your innovation team.

Now, if you asked me which questions I'd ask if I were interviewing someone tomorrow, I might draw some inspiration from an old party game that dates back to the 1800s: Twenty Questions.[1]

You may have played it yourself. The idea is that a person thinks of a someone or a something and the rest of the group gets to ask twenty questions to see if they can figure out the who or what. With that spirit in mind, I'm offering up the twenty questions I'd start with if I were trying to determine whether someone had an innovator's spirit. Keep in mind, these questions are just a starting point. They're a way to look past someone's resume and get a glimpse into who they are, what they believe, and how they will likely behave in your organization. These are ideas that have worked for me, but they are not a recipe. Remember that there is always something better—so make them your own.

Twenty Questions to Help Uncover the Innovator's Spirit

1. Innovation is something new, something that has never been done before. It is making the impossible possible. So what is the first step in the pursuit of the impossible?

2. Innovation is really hard. It is filled with more failure than success. Why do you want to pursue innovation?

3. What is your favorite innovation? Why?

4. Do you believe that Apple is innovative? Why or why not?

5. What is the difference between management and leadership? Why do you think the list of best-managed companies does not overlap with the list of most innovative companies?

6. How do you react when you lose? How does it make you feel? What do you do next?

7. You are a consultant. One day, your client, a tire manufacturer, tells you they've invented a new tire that lasts for more than one hundred thousand miles. It would reduce the demand for tires by five to ten times. What would you advise them to do with this invention?

8. If you could make two decisions in a month and get them both right, or make ten decisions and get seven wrong, which would you do? Why? Is that what you've really done in the past?

9. Which is more effective for coming up with the best new ideas: a brainstorming session or a debate? How would you react if someone told you your idea was stupid?

10. How do you strike the balance between telling your boss the brutal truth and making them feel like you have everything under control?

11. How do you use consensus to drive innovation?

12. What is your biggest failure? Who did you tell about your failure? What would you do differently the next time?

13. Is a crisis good or bad for innovation?

14. How do you get customer insight on an innovative new idea—something they've never seen or experienced before?

15. If you were going to start a company to compete against your current company, what would you do? Why haven't you done it already?

16. Give me an example of when you thought outside the box. Was the box real or imagined?

17. If you stand back and think about the world today, which business or industry do you believe is most in need of innovation?

18. Have you ever had a rival in your life? How did it affect your motivation?

19. How important is your job title to you? Do you need a certain title to be successful in this role?

20. How would you estimate the circumference of the earth without looking it up? Please walk me through your estimate—right here and now.

Acknowledgments

THE IDEAS IN THIS BOOK were many years in the making and I want to thank everyone that has been a part of this incredible journey. Innovation is a team sport and I have been very fortunate to have great teammates along the way.

I want to thank the founders of Cree, who not only had the courage to start a company to develop technology that nobody else thought would be commercially viable but also had the drive to keep going despite many challenges along the way. I sincerely appreciate the opportunity you gave me to join the team and to find my innovator's spirit. Many of the best ideas in this book came from watching you, and if I got anything wrong, I'm sure you will let me know.

To the many great innovators at Cree: Your ability to find new ways to solve problems and develop truly innovative technology is second to none. You constantly proved that anything is possible if you set your mind to it and are willing to work hard enough.

This book is my attempt to describe some of the unique beliefs and behaviors that made our strategy of innovation work. Thank you for answering my many questions and always keeping me true to our mission.

To the people who worked directly for me and served on the Cree leadership team over the years: I'm sure you will recognize many of these ideas, because we developed them together. We built a great company, and you deserve much of the credit. Thank you for your time, energy, and dedication to making the impossible possible.

To the thousands of Cree employees around the world who helped take new ideas and turn them into innovations: It was a pleasure to work with all of you and an honor to represent you as CEO for over sixteen years. Thank you for your energy, enthusiasm, and commitment to finding a better way and developing products that changed the world. Don't ever settle for good enough.

I want to thank Laura, my assistant for many years, although it's not clear who was really in charge. I appreciate you trusting me and embracing the job description to "anticipate the un-anticipatable." I couldn't have done the job for as long as I did without your support and encouragement.

I want to thank Kris, Kate, Andrea, and the team at Marquette University that encouraged me to write this book. I would have never attempted this project without your support, and I would have given up early on without your encouragement. I hope you find the content helpful as you continue to develop the next generation of innovative leaders. I continue to strive to *Be the Difference.*

I want to thank Darren Dahl, who was my writing partner in this effort. This book simply wouldn't have been possible without your skill and expertise. You are a very talented writer that I also now consider to be a friend. You were able to help turn my ideas and stories into writing that is actually interesting to read. And you helped find additional stories to enable me to further illustrate the concepts. I will miss our many calls and discussions about which companies are truly innovative. I enjoyed the process so much that I'm hoping we get a chance to write another book together someday.

I want to thank the team at Greenleaf Book Group for your expertise and guidance on the book publishing process. From editing to production to branding, your advice was integral to creating a truly professional book. Lindsey, Tyler, Judy, Sam, and Justin—you were all a pleasure to work with.

I want to thank Charles Ries, who read my initial book proposal and told me that I needed to show the reader, not tell the reader. I kept your advice in mind every day as I wrote the book.

I want to thank Dr. Gerald Bell, whose wisdom and coaching helped me understand both my team and myself in ways that were critical to my development as a leader.

I want to thank Rob, Lauren, Al, Kate, Andrea, Scott, Zach, and Kyle for the many hours you spent reading drafts along the way. Your feedback was invaluable and made the book far better.

I've learned that much of who we are comes from how we grow up. I was fortunate to be part of a large family. My parents created a loving environment that challenged us to strive for excellence and gave us the freedom to figure things out on our own. As the fifth of six kids, I learned how to compete and developed a range of people skills that have been very useful later in life. Thank you to my family for all of your support over the years and pushing me to strive for better.

I would like to thank my children, Kim, Kelly, and Chuckie, for their support and input on the book. I know you saw some of these concepts in action firsthand as you were growing up. Thanks for being so patient with me as your father and I'm sorry for all of the time together that I missed while traveling around the world on business. I hope you each find your own innovator's spirit and remember that you can do anything you set your mind to.

Most important, I'd like to thank my wife, Karen. You have been my best friend for almost thirty-five years. None of this would have been possible without your support and encouragement. Thank you for reading the many drafts along the way. I appreciate your insight, feedback, and friendship more than you will ever know.

Index

Notes

CHAPTER ONE

1. Tina Gose, "Nikola Tesla vs. Thomas Edison: Who Was the Better Inventor?," *Live Science*, July 10, 2014.

2. Curt Schleier, "Thomas Edison's Imagination Lit Up The Modern World," *Investors.com*, September 28, 2015.

3. Christopher Klein, "When Edison Turned Night into Day," *History*, December 17, 2014.

4. Randy Alread, "Oct. 21, 1879: Edison Gets the Bright Light Right," *Wired*, October 21, 2009.

5. Mark Essig, *Edison and the Electric Chair* (New York: Walker & Company, 2003), loc. 550, Kindle version.

6. Essig, *Edison.*

7. Klein, "Edison."

8. Later on, ironically, Edison's own company—which eventually merged with the Thomson-Houston Electric Company to become the General Electric Company in a deal financed by J. P. Morgan—embraced Tesla's AC power as a way to compete against Westinghouse in the race to electrify the country.

9. Joseph J. Ellis, *Founding Brothers: The Revolutionary Generation* (New York: Alfred A. Knopf, 2000), 130.

10. Ellis, *Founding Brothers*, 130.

11. Ellis, *Founding Brothers*, 130.

CHAPTER TWO

1. Peter Drucker, *The Essential Drucker*, reissue ed. (New York: HarperCollins e-books, October 13, 2009), loc. 260, Kindle.

CHAPTER THREE

1. Guy Kawasaki, "Guy Kawasaki: Evangelist in Chief," interview by Charles Trevail, *Outside In* (podcast), March 24, 2019.
2. Jonah Lehrer, "Groupthink: The Brainstorming Myth," *The New Yorker*, January 30, 2012.
3. Oliver Staley, "Silicon Valley's Confrontational Management Style Started with Andy Grove," *Quartz*, March 22, 2016.
4. Tobi Lütke, "From Snowboard Shop to Billion-Dollar Company," interview by Tim Ferriss, *The Tim Ferriss Show* (podcast), February 7, 2019.
5. Trevor Cole, "Our Canadian CEO of the Year You've Probably Never Heard of," *The Globe and Mail*, May 12, 2018.
6. Ed Catmull and Amy Wallace, *Creativity, Inc.* (Random House, 2014), loc. 1370–1371, Kindle.
7. Kawasaki, interview.
8. David Burkus, "How Criticism Creates Innovative Teams," *Harvard Business Review*, September 20, 2013.

CHAPTER FOUR

1. David McCullough, *The Wright Brothers* (New York: Simon & Schuster, 2015), 34.
2. McCullough, *The Wright Brothers*, 8.
3. McCullough, *The Wright Brothers*, 106.
4. Rod Canion, "Compaq Computers: Rod Canion," interview by Guy Raz, *How I Built This* (podcast), NPR, May 22, 2017.
5. John Carreyrou, "Hot Startup Theranos Has Struggled With Its Blood-Test Technology," *The Wall Street Journal*, October 16, 2015.
6. John Carreyrou, *Bad Blood: Secrets and Lies in a Silicon Valley Startup* (New York: Knopf, 2018).

CHAPTER FIVE

1. Apocryphally attributed to Einstein; https://quoteinvestigator. com/2017/09/02/clutter.

2. I learned the story by watching an excellent miniseries about the company's start called *Harley and the Davidsons:* https://www.discovery.com/tv-shows/ harley-and-the-davidsons.

3. Margie Siegal, *Harley-Davidson: A History of the World's Most Famous Motorcycle* (London: Shire Publications, 2014), loc. 43, Kindle.

4. Siegal, *Harley-Davidson.*

5. Harley-Davidson, https://www.harley-davidson.com/us/en/museum/explore/ hd-timeline.html.

6. Scott Smith, "How Harley-Davidson's Founders Hogged the Motorcycle Market," *Investor's Business Daily*, August 4, 2017.

7. Smith, "Harley-Davidson's Founders."

8. Kathleen D. Vohs, "It's Not 'Mess.' It's Creativity," *The New York Times*, September 13, 2013.

9. https://www.sciencehistory.org/historical-profile/alexander-fleming.

10. Howard Market, "The Real Story Behind Penicillin," *PBS*, September 27, 2013.

11. https://charlesgoodyear101.weebly.com/vulcanized-rubber.html.

12. "The Charles Goodyear Story," Goodyear.com, reprinted from *Reader's Digest*, January 1958, https://corporate.goodyear.com/en-US/about/history/charles-goodyear-story.html.

13. Clive Cookson, "Pharma Industry's Return on R&D Investment Falls Sharply," *The Financial Times*, December 13, 2017; Ben Hirschler, "Pharma Industry Returns on R&D Investment Hit 9-Year Low," *Reuters*, December 18, 2018.

14. Hirschler, "Pharma Industry"; "Embracing the Future of Work to Unlock R&D Productivity," Deloitte, https://www2.deloitte.com/us/en/pages/life-sciences-and-health-care/articles/measuring-return-from-pharmaceutical-innovation.html.

15. Clifton Leaf, "How Stale Is Innovation in Drug Discovery? Think: 5-Year-Old Yogurt," *Fortune*, March 6, 2018.

16. Standish Fleming, "Pharma's Innovation Crisis, Part 1: Why The Experts Can't Fix It," *Forbes*, September 6, 2018.

17. http://metacool.com/metacool-innovation-principle-18.

18. Jacob Ganz, "The Truth about Van Halen and Those Brown M&Ms," *NPR*, February 14, 2012.

CHAPTER SIX

1. Apocryphally credited to Lincoln; https://quoteinvestigator.com/2012/09/27/invent-the-future.

2. Jim Koch, *Quench Your Own Thirst* (New York: Flatiron Books, 2016), loc. 205, Kindle.

3. Koch, *Quench Your Own Thirst*, loc. 244.

4. Koch, *Quench Your Own Thirst*, loc. 255.

5. Koch, *Quench Your Own Thirst*, loc. 43.

6. Koch, *Quench Your Own Thirst*, loc. 257.

7. Koch, *Quench Your Own Thirst*, loc. 278.

8. Ashlee Vance, *Elon Musk: Tesla, SpaceX, and the Quest for a Fantastic Future* (New York: Ecco, 2015), 149.

9. Vance, *Elon Musk,* 152.

10. Vance, *Elon Musk,* 155.

11. Vance, *Elon Musk,* 155.

12. Quincy Larson, "Linux Is 25. Yay! Let's Celebrate with 25 Stunning Facts about Linux," *Medium*, August 28, 2016.

13. Larson, "Linux Is 25."

CHAPTER SEVEN

1. Blake Morgan, "A Global View of 'The Customer Is Always Right,'" *Forbes*, September 24, 2018.

2. Henry Ford, *My Life and Work: The Autobiography of Henry Ford* (New York: Doubleday, 1922), 21.

3. The quote "you don't need a quarter-inch drill bit, you need a quarter-inch hole" belongs to Theodore Levitt, an American economist and professor at Harvard Business School. He wrote *Marketing Myopia* and *Marketing for Business Growth*. He was also quoted as saying: "Creativity thinks up new things. Innovation does new things. The difference speaks for itself. Yet the fluent advisers to business seldom make the distinction. They tend to rate ideas more by their novelty than by their practicability."

4. Pablo Sánchez Kohn, "Steve Jobs on Market Research #MRX," YouTube, April 24, 2016, https://www.youtube.com/watch?v=Bc1NAi8AG68.

5. Howard Yu, "Google's Carpool Pilot with Waze Offers Lessons for Innovative Executives," *Forbes*, September 4, 2016.

6. W. Chan Kim and Renée Mauborgne, *Blue Ocean Strategy: How to Create*

Uncontested Market Space and Make Competition Irrelevant (Boston: Harvard Business Review Press, 2005), loc. 3485, Kindle.

7. Greg Toppo, "Curtain Falls on Final Ringling Bros. Circus Performance," *USA Today*, May 21, 2017.

8. Kim and Mauborgne, *Blue Ocean Strategy*, loc. 434.

9. Kim and Mauborgne, *Blue Ocean Strategy*, loc. 440.

10. Nathan McAlone, "Here's How Uber Got Its Start and Grew to Become the Most Valuable Startup in the World," *Business Insider,* September 13, 2015.

11. Morgan Brown, "Airbnb: The Growth Story You Didn't Know," GrowthHackers, 2015, https://growthhackers.com/growth-studies/airbnb.

CHAPTER EIGHT

1. Daniel Alef, *Igor I. Sikorsky: Big Dreams, Big Planes, and the Rise of Helicopters* (Santa Barbara, CA: Titans of Fortune, 2011), loc. 92, Kindle.

2. Alef, *Igor I. Sikorsky*, loc. 107.

3. Alef, *Igor I. Sikorsky*, loc. 224.

4. Alef, *Igor I. Sikorsky*, loc. 339.

5. Alef, *Igor I. Sikorsky*, loc. 361.

6. Alef, *Igor I. Sikorsky*, loc. 365.

7. Alef, *Igor I. Sikorsky*, loc. 408.

8. Alef, *Igor I. Sikorsky*, loc. 457.

9. "Clarence Birdseye: A Chilling Discovery," *Entrepreneur*, October 16, 2008.

10. "Desi Arnaz & Lucille Ball," *Entrepreneur*, October 16, 2008.

11. "Fred Smith: An Overnight Success," *Entrepreneur*, October 16, 2008.

12. Tendayi Viki, "On the Fifth Anniversary of Kodak's Bankruptcy, How Can Large Companies Sustain Innovation?," *Forbes*, January 19, 2017.

13. National Museum of Natural History, "Original Kodak Camera, Serial No. 540," https://americanhistory.si.edu/collections/search/object/nmah_760118.

14. Pete Pachal, "How Kodak Squandered Every Single Digital Opportunity It Had," *Mashable*, January 20, 2012.

15. Pachal, "Kodak Squandered."

16. James Estrin, "Kodak's First Digital Moment," *The New York Times*, August 12, 2015.

17. Estrin, "Kodak's First."

18. Viki, "Kodak's Bankruptcy."

19. Viki, "Kodak's Bankruptcy."

CHAPTER NINE

1. "Woman Invented Dishwasher," U.S. Patent and Trademark Office, December 27, 2001, https://www.uspto.gov/about-us/news-updates/woman-invented-dishwasher.

2. J. M. Fenster, "The Woman Who Invented the Dishwasher," *Invention and Technology 15*, no. 2 (Fall 1999), https://www.inventionandtech.com/node/86034.

3. Fenster, "The Woman."

4. Fenster, "The Woman."

5. Abigail Hess, "Harvard Business School Professor: Half of American Colleges Will Be Bankrupt in 10 to 15 Years," *CNBC*, August 30, 2018.

6. Carol Dweck, *Mindset: The New Psychology of Success* (New York: Random House, 2006), 3.

7. Dweck, *Mindset*, 4.

8. Dweck, *Mindset*, 7.

9. Barack Obama, interview with Marc Maron, *WTF Podcast with Marc Maron*, #613 HQ/HD, 2015, https://www.youtube.com/watch?v=gAnMYuQhocE.

10. Bill Gates, *Business @ the Speed of Thought: Using a Digital Nervous System* (New York: Hatchette Book Group, 1999), loc. 3563, Kindle.

11. Gates, *Business*, loc. 2524.

12. Gates, *Business*, loc. 2531.

13. Nicholas Jasinski, "How Amazon Is Disrupting These 6 Sectors," *Barron's*, October 11, 2018.

14. Brad Stone, *The Everything Store: Jeff Bezos and the Age of Amazon* (New York: Little, Brown and Company, 2013), loc. 370, Kindle.

15. Amazon SEC filing Exhibit 99.1: https://www.sec.gov/Archives/edgar/data/1018724/000119312516530910/d168744dex991.htm.

16. Eugene Kim, "How Amazon CEO Jeff Bezos Has Inspired People to Change the Way They Think about Failure," *Business Insider*, May 28, 2016.

17. Jillian D'Onfro, "Jeff Bezos: Why It Won't Matter If the Fire Phone Flops," *Business Insider*, December 2, 2014.

18. Kim, "Amazon."

19. https://www.sec.gov/Archives/edgar/data/1018724/000119312516530910/d168744dex991.htm.

CHAPTER TEN

1. Apocryphally attributed to Einstein; https://quoteinvestigator. com/2012/10/18/follows-crowd.

2. Barbara Goldsmith, *Obsessive Genius: The Inner World of Marie Curie* (New York: W. W. Norton & Company, 2005), loc. 101, Kindle.

3. Goldsmith, *Obsessive Genius*, loc. 963.

4. Goldsmith, *Obsessive Genius*, loc. 955.

5. Goldsmith, *Obsessive Genius*, loc. 1004.

6. Goldsmith, *Obsessive Genius*, loc. 160.

7. Goldsmith, *Obsessive Genius*, loc. 2083.

8. GoodReads.com: https://www.goodreads.com/ quotes/64597-all-truths-are-easy-to-understand-once-they-are-discovered.

9. Nola Taylor Redd, "Galileo Galilei: Biography, Inventions & Other Facts," *Space.com*, November 14, 2017.

10. Walmart history: https://corporate.walmart.com/our-story/our-history.

11. Sam Walton with John Huey, *Sam Walton: Made in America* (New York: Bantam Books, 1993), 317.

12. Walton with Huey, *Sam Walton*, 29.

13. Walton with Huey, *Sam Walton*, 31.

14. Walton with Huey, *Sam Walton*, 34.

15. Walton with Huey, *Sam Walton*, 50.

16. Walton with Huey, *Sam Walton*, 45.

17. Walton with Huey, *Sam Walton*, 80.

18. "Southwest Airlines Reports Fourth Quarter and Annual Profit; 46th Consecutive Year of Profitability," Southwest, January 24, 2019, http://investors.southwest.com/news-and-events/news-relea ses/2019/01-24-2019-113106440.

19. Kevin and Jackie Freiberg, *Nuts!: Southwest Airlines' Crazy Recipe for Business and Personal Success* (New York: Broadway Books, 1997), 36.

20. Freiberg and Freiberg, *Nuts!*, 130.

21. Shannon Van Sant, "Southwest Airlines Says It Will Stop Serving Peanuts," July 10, 2019. Southwest is now one of the first airlines to stop handing them out to help protect customers with allergies. You can still get free pretzels.

22. Freiberg and Freiberg, *Nuts!*, 33.

CHAPTER ELEVEN

1. Meg Busse, "Experimentation: A Shortcut to Innovation," *Stanford Social Innovation Review*, April 1, 2014.

2. John Eisenberg, *That First Season: How Vince Lombardi Took the Worst Team in the NFL and Set It on the Path to Glory* (Boston: Houghton Mifflin Harcourt, 2009), loc. 582, Kindle.

3. Eisenberg, *That First Season*, loc. 1218.

4. Buster Olney, "Pro Football; Instant Pictures Help Giants Gain a Different Perspective," *The New York Times,* December 21, 2002.

5. Eisenberg, *That First Season*, loc. 651.

6. Eisenberg, *That First Season*, loc. 1211.

7. Michael J. de la Merced, "Walmart to Buy Bonobos, Men's Wear Company, for $310 Million," *The New York Times*, June 16, 2017.

8. Andy Dunn, "Bonobos: Andy Dunn," interview by Guy Raz, *How I Built This* (podcast), NPR, January 21, 2019.

9. Dunn, interview.

10. Ilan Mochari, "The Secret to Retail Success? No Stock or Inventory," *Inc.*, March 14, 2016.

11. Dunn, interview.

12. Dunn, interview.

13. Dunn, interview.

14. Terrance Ross, "Bonobos Founder Shares His Success Story, Advice for Entrepreneurs," *USA Today*, June 29, 2012.

15. https://www.agilealliance.org/agile101/the-agile-manifesto.

16. Eric Ries, *The Lean Startup* (New York: Currency, 2011), 9.

17. Susan Wojcicki, "The Eight Pillars of Innovation," ThinkWithGoogle, July 2011, https://www.thinkwithgoogle.com/marketing-resources/8-pillars-of-innovation.

18. Enrique Dans, "Here's the Problem with Google's Innovation Strategy," *Forbes*, April 4, 2019.

19. David Silver, "Don't Throw Rocks at the Google Self-Driving Cars," *Forbes*, January 3, 2019.

20. Alicia Kort, "The Story of Steve Jobs, Xerox and Who Really Invented the Personal Computer," *Newsweek*, March 19, 2016.

CHAPTER TWELVE

1. Henry S. F. Cooper Jr., *Thirteen: The Apollo Flight That Failed* (New York: Open Road Media, 2013), 106.

2. Cooper, *Thirteen*, 41.

3. Cooper, *Thirteen*, 153.

4. Samuel B. Griffith, *Sun Tzu: The Art of War* (London: Oxford University Press, 1963), 134.

5. Griffith, *Sun Tzu*, 134.

6. Jim Collins, "A Rare Interview with a Reclusive Polymath," interview by Tim Ferriss, *The Tim Ferriss Show* (podcast), #361, February 16, 2019.

7. Ashley Rodriguez, "Ten Years Ago, Netflix Launched Streaming Video and Changed the Way We Watch Everything," *Quartz*, January 17, 2017.

8. Nick Wingfield and Brian Stelter, "How Netflix Lost 800,000 Members, and Good Will," *The New York Times,* October 24, 2011.

9. Cynthia Littleton, "Ted Sarandos on How Netflix Predicted the Future of TV," *Variety*, August 21, 2018.

10. Greg Petraetis, "How Netflix Built a House of Cards with Big Data," *CIO.com*, July 13, 2017.

11. Christopher To, Gavin Kilduff, Lisa D. Ordóñez, and Maurice E. Schweitzer, "Research: We Take More Risks When We Compete Against Rivals," *Harvard Business Review*, July 17, 2018.

12. To et al., "Research."

13. Laura Entis, "3 Ways to Use a Rivalry to Increase Your Business Performance," *Entrepreneur*, December 4, 2014.

14. Entis, "3 Ways."

15. Adam Grant, "The Creative Power of Misfits," *WorkLife* (podcast), March 5, 2019.

16. Grant, "Creative Power of Misfits."

17. Grant, "Creative Power of Misfits."

18. Grant, "Creative Power of Misfits."

19. Adam Grant, "Frustrated at Work? That Might Just Lead to Your Next Breakthrough," *The New York Times*, March 8, 2019.

20. Grant, "Frustrated at Work?"

AUTHOR'S NOTE

1. Mansfield Tracy Walsworth, *Twenty Questions: A Short Treatise on the Game* (New York: Henry Holt & Co., 1882).

About the Author

CHUCK SWOBODA is the Innovator-in-Residence at Marquette University, President of Cape Point Advisors, and the retired Chairman and CEO of Cree, Inc. During his time with Cree, the company led the LED Lighting Revolution that drove the obsolescence of the Edison light bulb. He is an author, speaker, and host of the *Innovators on Tap* podcast and has over thirty years of experience in the technology business. Chuck is also a co-inventor on twenty-five patents covering LED and lighting-related technology.

In 2010, Chuck was named Ernst & Young's Entrepreneur of the Year for the Carolinas. During his time as CEO, Cree was recognized as *MIT Technology Review*'s 50 Smartest Companies for 2014 and as one of *Fast Company*'s World's 50 Most Innovative Companies in 2015.

Chuck is passionate about innovation, leadership, and craft beer. He serves on the boards of several companies and is part owner of Lonerider Brewing Company. He and his wife are committed